Brothers
2011
love,
Annemarie

COOL, CALM & CONTENTIOUS

COOL, CALM
&
CONTENTIOUS

Merrill Markoe

VILLARD ⓥ NEW YORK

Published in the United States by Villard Books, an imprint of
The Random House Publishing Group, a division of
Random House, Inc., New York.

VILLARD BOOKS and VILLARD & "V" CIRCLED Design are registered
trademarks of Random House, Inc.

Grateful acknowledgment is made to George Meyer to reprint an
excerpt from "Gone, All Gone" by George Meyer. Reprinted by
permission of the author.

Library of Congress Cataloging-in-Publication Data
Markoe, Merrill.
Cool, calm & contentious / Merrill Markoe.
p. cm.
ISBN 978-0-345-51891-0
eBook ISBN 978-0-345-51893-4
1. Markoe, Merrill. 2. Markoe, Merrill—Childhood and youth.
3. Markoe, Merrill—Humor. 4. Writers, American—20th century—
Biography. I. Title. II. Title: Cool, calm and contentious.
PS3563.A6652Z46 2011
813'.54—dc22   2011028395

Printed in the United States of America on acid-free paper

www.villard.com

2 4 6 8 9 7 5 3 1

First Edition

Book design by Susan Turner

CONTENTS

COOL, CALM & CONTENTIOUS

The Place, the Food, Everything Awful: The Diaries of Ronny Markoe

FOR MOST OF HER LIFE, MY MOTHER WAS VARYING DEGREES OF pissed off. And not just at me. She was pissed off at everyone. But the conspicuous absence of colorful, controversial political and literary figures and/or captains of industry at our dinner table caused me to take the brunt of it.

It was hard to trace her hostility to its origin because she wasn't introspective. If you asked her why she was so mad, which I often did, she would say that she *told* you *on several occasions* to put your dishes in the dishwasher or to *change that horrible shirt*. That was as deep as it got.

It probably didn't help that my mother didn't feel well a lot of the time, afflicted with a wide variety of symptoms, many of which I associated with her always simmering rage. The first time I remember her being hospitalized was when I was in the third grade. We had just moved from New Jersey to Florida. I was sitting on the floor, in the midst of a one-person jacks-playing marathon, when the phone rang. It was her sister-in-law, calling long-distance from New York. I watched all the color drain from my mother's face as she began to comprehend that her brother had dropped dead of a heart attack at the age of thirty-three.

Not emotionally up to the responsibility of informing my grandmother, who lived with us, that her only son was dead, my mother instead pretended that her brother had survived, then put my grandmother on a plane to New York to go visit him in the hospital. This she confessed to me a couple of hours later, while sobbing uncontrollably during a harrowing drive home from the airport as I kept my hands hovering over hers on the steering wheel, terrified of finding myself, at the age of eight, in charge of a runaway vehicle that was careening into other cars on its way to the middle of a freeway median strip.

A few days later, my mother was diagnosed with ulcerative colitis and hospitalized for two weeks.

From that point on, she never left the house for any extended period, even a weekend, without what she called her "train case": a portable pharmacy, about the size of a bread box, made of hard white plastic with a handle on top. It opened into many compartments, most of them full of amber-colored prescription bottles. Inside, she always had prednisone, in case of an uncomfortable intestinal flare-up, along with a couple kinds of painkillers—Darvon, Tylenol with codeine, Vicodin, paregoric—as well as Imodium, Kaopectate, Lomotil, Elavil, and those old standbys Valium and Xanax. In addition to her abdominal discomfort, she was constantly being treated for other unidentifiable inflammations: pains in her arms, legs, ankles, neck, and back; swellings, skin eruptions, allergies. For the rest of her life, whenever I saw her on holidays or birthdays, she was either coming down with something or recuperating from something else.

Maybe she would have had medical problems even if she'd had a sunny disposition, but it seems just as possible to me that her endless physical problems may have been worsened by her seething, unacknowledged, and unexamined rage. It's also possible that she was set at a permanent rolling boil by her own utterly dependent and anxiety-ridden widowed mother, who moved in with her on the eve of her marriage to my father, then refused to get a job, learn to drive, or move to a nearby apartment when my father offered to pay for one, all the while maintaining an oblivious attitude centered around the premise that she was only there to help. That could have played a role in pissing my mother off.

It certainly would have gotten to me.

By all accounts, my mother started life as a pretty, brighter than average Brooklyn kid who skipped a lot of grades and went off to college at fifteen.

The few photos of her from this period show a cocky, fashionable girl of the 1930s, operating in the stylistic middle ground between Lauren Bacall and Dorothy Parker. She had shoulder-length, light brown, wavy hair that she wore swept up in a pompadour style, sometimes with a flower tucked coquettishly behind one ear. In photographs, she always looked pleased with herself, radiating confidence. The people who grew up with her all mentioned her wisecracking air of sophistication, smartly accessorized with swearing, chain-smoking, and a large multilanguage vocabulary.

During her late teens and early twenties, she fancied herself a worldly adventuress. By World War II, fresh out of college at nineteen, she'd gotten a job writing for a girlie magazine, a risqué credential she wore like a badge of honor. She loved to tell stories about how it was her job to come up with captions full of puns and wordplay that were then used under black-and-white photos of nude women posing behind beach balls and umbrellas.

When that ended, she did some copyediting for *Time,* followed by some graduate work in Mandarin Chinese at Columbia. The highlight of this phase seemed to be during the war, when she was written up in Earl Wilson's column in the *New York Post* after some woman saw her studying her Chinese-language textbook on the subway and reported her to the police as a Japanese spy. That was a big feather in the imaginary fedora of the glamorous trench-coat-wearing foreign-correspondent alter ego my mother carried around in her head. "Chinese is the coming language," Earl Wilson quoted my mother as saying.

But when the war ended, she didn't pursue any of the careers for which she'd been gearing herself up. Instead, she married my father, a man so controlled and methodical that he took an hour to dice a carrot and had a special pair of plastic sandals just to wear in the shower. Thus did my mother bid a fond farewell to her life as a foreign correspondent in order to stay home . . . and devote the next forty years to seething and being resentful.

Though she continued to think of herself as someone who lived for a rousing intellectual debate, she claimed to have found happiness with a man whose conversational digressions tended to be lengthy authoritative explanations of the obvious.* And though she insisted that she was blissfully wed, she often mentioned, over the years, that she was angry at my father because he didn't want any wife of his to work after they got married.

Looking back, it seems to me that she didn't fight this prefeminist battle as hard as she might have. My father was the kind of good sport who, despite initial signs of bluster, might have given in if she had argued passionately. If her work had been important enough to her, I always thought, my mother could have talked him into letting her pursue it. She also had no explanation for why, with her mother living on the premises, bored and available to watch the kids, she didn't at least pursue writing as a hobby.

Meanwhile, she continued to carry herself with a kind of calculated imperiousness . . . a Hillary Clinton–like bearing of a woman destined for literary greatness. She never stopped obsessing over word choice and sentence structure, never stopped chastising me for using slang. "Why do you have to say everything is 'neat,'" she would nag when I was in grade school, "when there are so many other magnificent words to choose from? Why not say, 'It's marvelous.' Or 'Bewitching!' Or 'Enchanting!' or 'Delightful!'" Though in my heart I suspected she was right, it was beyond embarrassing to imagine saying, "How delightful! Utterly enchanting!" to a group of my fellow fourth graders during a discussion of TV shows we liked.

---

*His detailed discourse delivered to my brother on the topic of "How to Fold a Napkin" remains to this day a classic of its kind. ("Hold both ends of the napkin out like so, one in each hand, and then shake the napkin until it is fully extended. . . .") It's also appropriate to note that on the occasion of the napkin seminar my brother was in his late thirties and had a Ph.D.

From junior high on, she would mark up all my homework papers with official copy editor's notations in blue pencil, the way she'd learned to at *Time*. (New paragraph! Stet! Sp!) She also took to carrying a marking pen with her when we went out, so she could circle and correct any misspellings when she found them in their natural habitat: in the grocery store (~~Avacadoe~~ Sp!), at the gas station (~~Gasolin~~ Sp!), at the drugstore (~~Asperine~~ Sp!).

Yet oddly enough, when later in life I wound up getting work as a writer, she never seemed especially pleased. She was in all ways a relentless and scrupulous cataloguer of my many shortcomings.

The minute I walked through the door of her house, I entered an already-in-progress pageant she was judging that had so many recently added unannounced categories it was impossible to be properly prepared. I was always too fat or too thin; my hair was too long, too shapeless, or too short; my clothes were too loose or too tight, too trendy or too adult, their colors too loud or too somber. If I became insulted, she became outraged.

"Do you want me to be less than honest?" she would say, as though tact were not also an option. If I argued a point or defended myself, she took offense at my audacity, because she was absolutely convinced that she was always right, including on occasions when she said things like "If someone acts like they're gay, that is a tip-off that they are not. Because why would they want you to know?" She would raise one eyebrow and say, "I don't happen to agree."

Next thing I knew, we would be in the middle of a fight. By the time I heard her shoes click click clicking down the hall as she stalked out of the room, I had given up trying to stand my ground. She either won or the fight would go on indefinitely.

One day, when I was in my thirties and gainfully employed as a writer on a television show, I decided to conduct an experiment. Knowing that I was going to have lunch with my mother later that day, I thought it would be interesting to see if I could achieve one perfect, criticism-free encounter. So I tried to predict all my own flaws and preemptively correct them. I bought a new outfit and a new pair of shoes, got an expensive haircut, and was careful with my makeup. I plucked my eyebrows to avoid a repeat of one particularly unpleasant family excursion to Mexico when my apparently slovenly and feeble attempts at eyebrow grooming pretty much ruined the whole vacation for everyone. Then, after I arrived at work, I made a stop at every office and cubicle on our floor and asked my co-workers to have a look at me and tell me if they noticed anything wrong.

"You look great," they all said. Or "That's a nice jacket." Or "You look so pretty all dressed up!"

When no one seemed able to highlight any obvious problem areas, I made them all work harder.

"No," I said. "Look again. There is definitely something wrong, and it won't take my mother five seconds to find it."

"You look good," they repeated.

"Are you sure?" I countered. "I bet there's something you're missing."

And of course, they all failed me. Within a minute of my entrance into my mother's hotel room, practically before she finished saying hello, she spotted a plastic loop that had once held a tag of some kind, lolling around on the underside of my brand-new purse.

"Come here," she said. "You've got a tag hanging off of your handbag."

I looked at my mother and thought, *Wow. You are good at this.*

Now that there is a period at the end of her sentence, it occurs to me that the only time I ever saw my mother happy was a few years before she died, when she went back to school and got her master's degree in librarianship. For a while, she rode around on a bookmobile, but by her mid-fifties, she'd found a job at Stanford University, helping to catalogue their library inventory on computer. For those few years, I noticed a positive shift in her demeanor—a certain lightheartedness had seeped in that had been missing before. And it lasted right up until my father, who was nearing retirement and wanted to do a lot of traveling, demanded that my mother quit her job in the interest of keeping him happy.

By sixty-five she was dead.

During one of her last medical emergencies my mother was encouraged to join a wellness group, where she reluctantly took part in an activity she had always belittled: group therapy. I had tried on and off for years to get her to consider talking to someone, maybe even begin taking an antidepressant. But she was as firmly against therapy as she was against exercise and, as always, once she had a final thought on the matter, there was no more room for discussion.

"How can a complete stranger claim to know anything

about me? Am I not a unique individual?" she used to argue, in one fell swoop discounting the entire legacy of literature and psychology.

Now, after a particularly serious hospitalization, and a virtual intervention by the medical staff in charge of her recovery, she had been unable to turn the suggestion down. Thus she was playing along, however reluctantly.

"We were each asked to pick a stuffed animal that represents our inner child," she explained to me when I visited her in the hospital, holding up a medium-sized plush stuffed monkey with very long arms and a scowling expression. "This is Little Ronny." Then she looked at me, rolled her eyes, and threw the monkey across the room. "Fuck Little Ronny," she said.

But something must have shaken loose in those sessions, because not too long afterward, when she was finally back home, she and I talked intimately for the very first time. Unprompted by me, and totally unexpectedly, we had a long, rambling, two-way conversation that felt to me like a breakthrough in our relationship. For the first time we sounded like two friends.

"Mom," I said to her as the conversation was winding down, "I just want to say that I loved talking to you like this. I'm really glad we can talk to each other this way."

"Well, just because I'm talking to you like this now doesn't mean I *always* have to talk to you like this," she replied.

We never talked like that again.

At my mother's funeral the woman who ran her wellness group got up to give a speech. She was one of those down-to-earth, well-intentioned, sensible-looking women I associate with the San Francisco Bay Area—resplendent in woven materials, ethnic jewelry, and Birkenstocks. I was happy to see that she and the other people who had attended the wellness group, as well as the Stanford library people, seemed to feel genuine fondness for my mother. In a lovely impromptu speech, she talked about my mother's intelligence and her sense of humor. I found myself wishing there was video of the sessions so I could have a look at that for myself.

When I glanced over at my father, he was choking back tears, his face rigid with the sorrow he was restraining himself from showing.

Then the wellness lady decided to lead the assembled mourners in a visualization exercise to say goodbye.

"Imagine that you are someplace very beautiful," she said. "Pick a place you like. A place that makes you comfortable."

I imagined a beautiful grassy clearing in Tuolumne Meadows, above Yosemite Valley, where I used to go camping.

"Now find a place to sit down and wait for Ronny to come to you," she directed.

I visualized a redwood picnic table in the middle of that meadow, surrounded by tall green grass and wildflowers. I walked over to it and sat down on the wooden plank bench.

"Now imagine seeing Ronny. She comes toward you for the final time," said the wellness lady, and magically there she was: I actually saw my mother appear at the edge of the green, grassy area where the woods stopped and the meadow began. She was looking sharp in one of her matching knit pantsuits. Her short hair was light reddish blond and, as always, she was perfectly made-up. She looked immaculate, elegant, and sophisticated. She began to walk toward me.

This was not just another ephemeral visualization. This

was so uncannily realistic, I began to feel apprehensive, jittery, as I anticipated that something moving was about to occur. As my mother got closer, I could see the rouge on her cheeks and smell her cologne. I braced myself for a potentially embarrassing emotional explosion: loud noises, choking sobs, bottomless grief.

"Now she is with you, right beside you," the wellness lady said. "It is time to say your final farewell." And there she was in front of me: time to say goodbye to my mother. But before I could say a word, she spoke first.

"You've got to be joking," she said. "You don't mean to tell me that you expect me to sit down on this filthy picnic bench and get dirt all over my suit, do you? You must be kidding. And I hope you don't think I'm going to sit down on the grass. Those grass stains never come out."

Then I remembered, as someone who has earned a living as a scriptwriter, that a carefully drawn character always knows what it wants to say. A good writer respects that truth. Even at her mother's funeral.

There was only one more goodbye left.

A few days after the funeral, my father asked me to come home and help him sort through my mother's stuff. It was time to decide what to do with it all. So I put my sixty-pound, yellow German shepherd–mix mutt, Stan, into my old Honda Accord and drove up the coast to my parents' home near Palo Alto.

The house looked the same when I first entered, but the air was a lot more still. A giant presence was missing.

Walking into the bedroom my father and mother shared,

I found it disturbing to be allowed full access to her private domain. But on my father's instructions, I began to look through her jewelry box and chest of drawers for the first time. Every garment she owned was carefully ironed and in tip-top condition. The aggregate stuff, pushed together in several crowded closets, stood as a collective monument to the thousands of arguments my mother and I had had over the years about my taste in clothes. Try as I might, I couldn't find a way to want to add any of her double-knit pantsuits or polyester floral print blouses to my existing wardrobe of T-shirts and jeans.

As I was creating a pile of clothing to give to the Salvation Army and Goodwill, I spotted something that provoked such a dramatic reaction in me it was almost as though it came with its own soundtrack by John Adams. There they were: a stack of diaries that my mother kept piled on the highest shelf of her closet. I had been looking at that tower of four-by-eight-inch diaries for years, watching it grow like some kind of mineral deposit or tiny condo complex; by the time my mother died, there were at least fifteen of them. Some had flower-patterned fabric covers and lined pages; some were black pebble board with unlined pages. Each one was labeled by year and countries visited, usually with a piece of paper my mother had cut out and taped to the spine. As an inveterate diary keeper myself, I'd always wondered about the contents of these books. Did my mother let her frustrations and true feelings show on these pages the way I had always done in mine? It felt a little bit indecent even picking the books up and holding them. Should I burn them and preserve her privacy forever?

But now that she was gone, they beckoned to me loudly. Perhaps I was meant to read them and uncover things she'd always wanted me to know but couldn't talk about comfortably.

I asked my father if he wanted to keep them, assuming he would say yes.

"Naaah," he said. "You want 'em? Take 'em. What the hell am I gonna do with 'em?"

I tried to imagine the enormousness of the life adjustment my dad was suddenly facing . . . forty years of marriage vaporized. Maybe more intimacy was too overwhelming for him right now?

Then it was time to make the seven-hour drive down the coast of California, back to my home in Los Angeles. With my dog Stan in the passenger seat beside me, and the diaries in a bag on the backseat, I rolled my old Honda down the long driveway of my parents' home. A kind of emotional terror swept over me. What secrets would the diaries reveal? Would she explain how she really felt about me? What if she had left behind evidence of a hidden other identity? If she really vented all her dark anger once and for all, could I handle her pain, her self-doubts, her fears? Or even more unnerving: What if she talked about her sex life with my dad? Could I handle that?

I'd never been sure of my mother's birth year, because she'd intentionally kept that hidden. But by every possible calculation, these diaries, which spanned 1959 through 1989, began when she was in her early thirties. Who was my mother back then?

As soon as I got home I poured myself a big glass of wine,

sat down on my sofa, and emptied the stack of diaries onto the cushions beside me. I took a deep breath, preparing to have a real talk with my mother for the very first time.

Before I got started, though, I decided to give my newly single dad a call to offer a little comfort and support.

"Dad, are you okay?" I said, after I heard him say hello. I was relieved by how normal his voice sounded.

"Listen, Merrill," he said, "I've just made myself a hot cup of coffee. I can't talk right now. My coffee will get cold." Then he hung up.

So that was that.

I decided to read the diaries in chronological order, starting with the multicolored floral-fabric-covered one dated May 6, 1959.

The opening entry began on the eve of their "first trip abroad on The Queen Mary." All of their relatives and friends had turned out for "a gay noisy Bon Voyage party. The Jeroboam of Piper Heidsieck champagne was gone in no time." I flinched a little at the use of the word "Jeroboam." It was so extremely Ronny Markoe. "Then we wandered aimlessly around the ship," she continued. "Tomorrow has the promise of adventure!"

How endearing! My mother, a girlish young wife . . . off to sea for the first time and seeking the promise of adventure! She sounded similarly energized a week later, on May 13, when she first encountered Switzerland. "What a sense of smallness is yours when you look out at the sheer glory of the Alps." How nice! She and my dad were having a good time, but not only that . . . did I detect a hint of self-reflection?

By May 20, I started to hear a more familiar voice:

ROME, MAY 20, 1959

Went to see Michelangelo's Moses at St. Peter's. So
dark in church could barely see. Then to Alfredo
Alfa Serofa for dinner. Looks like a Roman
SARDI's. Food was very tasty but service was so
quick you felt like you were being rushed. As I put
a last piece of lettuce in my mouth the waiter
rushed to remove my salad plate. Told him to go
away. As we ate a last piece of the main course, the
waiter asked (with our mouths still full) what we
wanted for dessert. I told him to go away and come
back in 5 minutes. I had scampi alla griglia which in
a better atmosphere at a slower tempo would have
tasted much better.

I kept reading and reading. From 1962 to 1988 my parents really got around. They went to every country in Europe, as well as Japan, China, and Africa. But not too many
ports of call escaped my mother's critical view.

MADRID, MAY 2, 1962

Madrid is a very large city, very bustling and not
very pretty. This morning about 11:00 we went to
see the Royal Palace, residence of the Spanish kings
until their deposure. Outside the building is ugly,
grey, forbidding, large and ornate. Inside we had,
along with others, an English speaking guide who
took us thru 30 of the most magnificent luxurious
living quarters I have ever seen . . . so breathtaking
that by the 30th room, your eyes have become dull

to beauty by its overabundance in too short a time. It's a relief to look at simple lines familiar to everyday life. Then we went to La Zambra Flamenco Dances performance. Saw true Flamenco troupe dancing. Was enjoyable although I don't care if I never see Flamenco dancing again. But the singing. Oy vay. That was for the birds.

LONDON, MAY 21, 1962

Arrived London and took airline bus to town—very long ride—and checked into Mt. Royal Hotel—huge old flea bag in Marble Arch area. Room was good sized but furniture old and dirty looking. Dust all over. Bathroom impossible. Person sitting on toilet could become double amputee if door was opened while performing. One closet only and that one too small for both Val-Pacs. Gerry completely disgusted. One bed broken. He's determined to stay only one night but I feel like I'm coming down with a cold. Throat is sore too. Took city tour of London. Drizzly weather. Guide unspeakably bad. Went to Carltontower Grill for roast beef and Yorkshire pudding. Food beautifully served but it certainly didn't taste like roast beef.

In October 1971, when she was in her mid-forties, she and my father took a month-long trip to Japan, Thailand, Singapore, Indonesia, and Bali. Amazingly enough, Japan got glowing reviews! "Just delicious and such a delightful experience can barely describe!" raved my mother. She was enamored of the Japanese people's cleanliness, politeness, formality, and artistic sense of design.

The other countries didn't fare as well.

CHENGMAI, THAILAND, THURSDAY, OCTOBER 21, 1971

At night we couldn't bear the idea of the restaurant at this hotel with its greasy dirty tablecloths and its filthy (albeit starched) napkins. At lunchtime they gave me a menu crawling with ants. Anyway we checked a book and decided to go to Sri Prackard for Chinese food. Well, that was the worst ever. The place, the food, everything awful. The menu had no prices and when the bill came it added up wrong. They tried to charge us for whisky we never had, for wash towels they gave us that we never used, but we made them itemize the bill and they backed down. We were so goddamned mad that we left no tip. Service was given us by the fat slob of an owner who took our order for lobster and served us shrimp. Then served us greasy chicken skin instead of chicken in the next dish. Finally we went to the Rincome Hotel. Oh the delight of a clean table and an unstained menu.

Bali really took a hit.

BALI BEACH HOTEL, SAT. OCT. 30, 1971

After the rain let up a bit, we visited the old palace, a series of low, old buildings that looked anything

but royal since they are currently being used as
souvenir shops, etc. Then we walked around the
town which was nice and muddy now from the
rains. It has no great charm. Just unpaved roads
lined with concrete buildings and open air stalls.
The streets are littered with refuse. The women are
not bare breasted at all, just very old women and
that is no sight of beauty. . . . The Balinese women
balance tremendous loads on their heads and
certainly have beautiful carriage but they're not as
lovely as I had thought. Certainly their dancing girls
are, but dancing girls the world over are the crème
de la crème. Old Balinese women are rarely still
graceful but mercilessly wrinkled . . . they look
terribly dried up and unattractive. The younger
women are work worn for the most part.

As my mother got older, she definitely did not get mel-
lower. Usually France was a reliable respite for her; she
prided herself on her ability to speak French and peppered
her everyday speech with phrases such as *Mon Dieu!* and *La
plus ça change* and *pied à terre*. Apparently 1976 was a bad year
for France.

FRANCE, MAY 1976
Drove through flat rather uninteresting countryside
for hours, interrupted by dreary little towns which
slowed our average speed way down to about 30
miles an hour. Gerry and I are both so tired that
we stopped, despite our original plans to push onto
Strasbourg, at a small town called Vitry-le-François.

Singularly uninteresting! The only game in town
was a weary looking "two bumper" called the Hotel
de la Pose where we checked into an even wearier
looking tiny room. We lunched at an open brasserie
on Niçoise salad and bad Alsatian wine. When we
sent the half carafe of wine back and asked for a
bottle of Riesling instead, the smart alec waiter
brought us an "open" bottle of Riesling which
tasted exactly like the wine we had just returned. I
scolded him and accused him of doing just that
(pouring the carafe wine into an already open
bottle) but he just shrugged and walked away. "We
were took." Went to bed early. Slept fitfully.

Two years later, Turkey let her down as well.

TURKEY, SAT. AP. 22, 1978
Dinner tonight was the usual slush: A tasteless soup,
a gluggy beef and rice dish and a Turkish sweet
(impossible to eat. It was doughy, wet baklava and
totally inedible). I was so exhausted I had the tray of
vile food sent to my room and here I am waiting.
This afternoon I took off from the group and went
walking on my own. I wasn't feeling too badly then
but the town nearby was nothing to see. Cheap little
stores full of items from the everyday world. The
hotel at Pamukkali was the worst one so far. It was
unclean and bitterly cold and no heat was sent up.
We went out poking around Cumhurryet Cadessi
with its dinky doo shops. The national costume of
Turkey seems to be flowered pantaloon pants and

white scarves over their heads. The women over 30 are either too fat or these shapeless pants make them seem that way.

Lest it appear that my mother's critiques were jingoistic, the country of her birth did not fare any better. This was a review from a two-week trip to the Southwest:

NEW MEXICO, SEPTEMBER 19, 1982
Our motel was "stashed" between 2 other ones, all jammed together. The 3 star AAA recommendation was anything but a find. We ate at the Red Lobster, across the street, and ordered King Crab legs. They were quite all right but the melted butter was salty as hell. And there was no getting sweet butter. Our waitress was very inexperienced. Just to get a small fork with which to pull out the crab meat was a reckoning that didn't happen until meal's end (along with a same time request for a nutcracker which also materialized after the need was gone). Turns out the Red Lobster is a chain. Never get a proper meal in a chain.

Finland took perhaps the biggest strafing of all. My mother shot the whole country down in flames.

HELSINKI, JUNE 30, 1985
Set out by car for the last leg of our Scandinavian journey. As usual, the scenery was unspectacular. Helsinki is a very commercial city with no

particular beauty, at least so far. Finland is not really the sort of country that offers a great deal to a tourist in the way of interesting places, foods, customs, architecture, music, in fact it is a most boring country. For me, and I think I speak for Gerry, we're just trying to find things to see and do to kill time for the Leningrad trip, and that may turn out to be something less than great since we couldn't get on a deluxe tour and from what I gather, anything less than deluxe is really second rate.

And yet Leningrad actually made them nostalgic for Helsinki!

LENINGRAD, JULY 2, 1985
Leningrad is a city of 4 to 5 story high old buildings and giant apartment complexes, square and Soviet in style...the whole town could use a coat of paint. Lunch was too awful to describe, except for the large lump of fat on my plate covered with gravy which I almost ate because I thought it must be fish of some sort.... Then we ran back to the bus and drove to the Hermitage Museum. Well! It was Sunday and the crowds were horrendous. Never really got to see much except from a distance. Then back to the hotel and into a bus to take us to the circus...a one-tent affair on hard benches and no air. No dancing bear! Just some acrobats, illusions, clowns making jokes in Russian, and undraped

females whirling assorted things. A dud.
TOMORROW WE GO BACK TO HELSINKI.
HOORAY!

And so it went. And went. I sat there on the couch, drinking wine, turning pages, waiting—in vain—for the painful introspection. What I found instead was a travelogue she had written for an imaginary audience, in which she presented herself as a globe-trotting sophisticate whose day began when she "breakfasted early and well." I was intimately acquainted with my mother's grandiose word choices. I do not recall being taught to use "breakfast" as a verb.

Who is she writing to? I began to wonder. *Was she thinking she might one day get these books published or just pretending that they had already been?* It was almost as if she had written a travel guide to advise other budget-conscious people of distinction, like herself, discriminating enough not to compromise their standards of perfection for the sake of momentary assimilation into some misguided second-rate foreign culture. And it was almost as if she took the shortcomings and discomforts of those other cultures as a personal affront.

There were no passages where she wondered about herself or her marriage or her kids. Yet she would fastidiously list the cost of every item she ate or bought or thought about eating or buying. Perhaps the entire country of Finland let her down, but she never failed to be utterly captivated by her own ability to make a sandwich.

"At about 11:30 just before we began a 125 mile stretch of desert road which did not indicate a single town in which to lunch we stopped at a real genuine dinky doo food emporium and I bought something with which to make sandwiches," my mother wrote on her journey through the American Southwest in 1982, clearly taken by a sense of herself as a rugged pioneer.

> A loaf of bread but no jug of wine, just Armour's beef bologna, a small package of American cheese, and a cucumber. Earlier in the trip at a cafeteria in Canyon de Chelly I had taken some give-away packets of mayonnaise and mustard. Now finally a week later they surely came in handy. Somewhere en route thru that desolate Nevada stretch of road I made Gerry a bologna and sliced cucumber sandwich laced with mayo and I ate a bologna and cheese and mustard with cucumber. I was making the sandwiches while he drove, using a paper bag on my lap for a cutting board and a pen knife to peel the cucumber and cut the sandwiches. For dessert Gerry had a piece of uneaten candy and a tin of apple juice and I had some icy cold water from my thermos. Gerry was hell bent on going, going. Finally we took 15 minutes to chomp away.

To be fair, my mother's diaries were not entirely joyless and scathing. There were passages of praise delivered whenever she encountered unassailable luxury. But her praise was hard-won. She wanted the reader to know that she was not easily duped; her educated understanding of the world could penetrate all attempts to fool her. She seemed to take pride in her ability to scratch the surface of beauty and find something disappointing lurking beneath. This was the writerly gift that she was willing to share with her myopic peers.

It might have been fun to talk to her about some of this. I would have liked to learn how her early years made her turn out this way. But her life was a topic about which she had no sense of humor. In her mind, she was one of the last of the clear-eyed uncompromised purists, the wizened survivor of countless fearlessly fought campaigns. For my mother to admit that she had flaws was for her to feel as though she were destroyed, transparent, nonexistent.

In this way she caused me to become her polar opposite. If perfection was both impossible and the only thing that mattered, then why mess with it at all? I turned into someone who not only reveled in my own imperfections but underlined them and paraded them like they were assets.

A former record executive in Los Angeles once told me about the day he had finally saved enough money to buy himself a new Porsche. When he took possession of it, its exquisite beauty so overwhelmed him that the only way he could feel comfortable enough to drive it was to first slowly back it into a wall and crease the rear bumper. I would be surprised if he was not raised by someone like my mother.

Unfortunately, there was nothing funny to my mother about the embracing of imperfections. She didn't even attend my high school graduation because I insisted on wearing a pair of shoes that did not match my dress.

For the first few years of college, I didn't finish a single creative project I started. The more I cared about the work, the less likely I was to complete it. If I declared the work finished, and someone (like my mother) "didn't happen to like it," then it would be deemed worthless and ruined forever. I was too afraid to allow someone to puncture my dream. I needed to retain the fantasy that I might add some amazing last-minute finishing touches that would have the power to deflect the eventual onslaught of negative criticism.

Maybe, in the last analysis, that was why my mother never pursued her career as a writer. Her own impossible standards were too tough on her. And it pissed her off.

When I finished reading her diaries, I did have a sense of completion. My lifelong problems of feeling judged by her and coming up short in all areas became both tolerable and funny. After all, I did no worse than the women of Bali. And possibly a little better than certain parts of Venice:

> We walked to St Mark's square and it is one of the most remarkable squares I have ever seen. And in terrible taste. So terribly overdecorated that its very bizarreness makes it almost beautiful.

In retrospect, it seems ludicrous that I spent the first half of my life seeking a positive review from someone who thought Piazza San Marco was in terrible taste. Though now that I think of it, finding the beauty in bizarreness has always been one of my passions. But which part of the thing was the beauty and which was the bizarre would have been one more thing about which my mother and I would have disagreed.

The best I could have hoped for, all things considered, was to receive the kind of review she gave to Charles Dickens when she was a student. In the margin of *The Dickens Reader*, one of her old hardbound college textbooks from the late 1930s that I had taken home with me as a memento, I found a remark in pencil, in my mother's distinctive handwriting. "Not one of his better works" she'd noted on the title page of *Oliver Twist*. "I was not impressed."

In Praise of Crazy Mommies

My mother to me: *"So is everything always a joke to you?"*

IN THE SUMMER OF 1977, WHEN I WAS IN MY MID-TWENTIES, I made the decision to switch professions from "artist/teacher" to "something in film or TV." While I was aware that my new plans were both risky and vague, I had been inspired by the filmmaking and scriptwriting classes I had audited at USC the previous year, where I'd had a job teaching painting and drawing to freshmen. I had also noticed that the paintings I was working on—the centerpiece of my career as I then saw it—were increasingly full of plot, language, and humor.

Branching out into a more dynamic form of expression seemed like an exciting next step. After some contemplation of what seemed like the possibilities for new employment, I concluded that the most viable point of entry for me might come through writing.

Though I had never worked as a writer before, I had a sense that it was something I could do, possibly from the years of grammar-related browbeating my mother had provided me. So I sat down and studied all the TV shows of that moment—viewing them for the first time as a possible meal ticket, focusing my attention on the ones I hated least. Then I spent a few months writing spec scripts for them, guided by the formulas for scriptwriting that I found in classes and books.

Once I was armed with a briefcase full of work that I hoped would get me a job, I packed up my car and prepared to make the drive from the Bay Area to Los Angeles. My plan, to the extent that I had one, was to give myself two months to see some results.

Right before I left, I stopped by my parents' house to spend the night. By now, I was well aware that neither of my parents thought much of my new vocation. My father's quote on the topic, if memory serves, was "Whaddya, nuts?"

And he was the more agreeable of the pair. Since I'd graduated college, my relationship to my mother had become so dicey that I had learned to limit the amount of time I spent with her to less than thirty-six hours. Somewhere between hour 24 and hour 36, I would see a minor change in her facial expression, a tiny flash around the eyes or an almost imperceptible tensing of the lip muscles. These were the early warning signs that she had begun shuffling through her Rolodex of my many shortcomings. But on this occasion, by only spending one night at their house, I figured I was a good twelve to eighteen hours ahead of our regularly scheduled fight. By my calculations, I would be somewhere around San Luis Obispo or Santa Barbara by the time the conflict erupted.

The three of us had a pleasant enough bon voyage dinner. And then afterward, born of an old habit not yet dead, I said yes when my mother asked me to show her a few of the scripts I was taking with me. Since she considered herself my mentor, as well an expert in all things involving the English language, her approval of my work seemed like an important milestone. So I handed her my most polished script and disappeared into my old bedroom, which by then had been converted into my mother's office. There I paced restlessly, feeling sick to my stomach as I waited for an official verdict.

About an hour later, I stopped by the living room to check on her reaction. She was sitting in her BarcaLounger, the script closed in her lap. I didn't know if she had heard me enter the room so I stood quietly, watching her stare into the middle distance, trying to read something in the way she was running her tongue over her front teeth and pursing her lips.

What was her lack of facial expression saying?

"So?" I finally said, when I could take it no more.

She looked over at me, raised her eyebrows, and shrugged. "Well, I don't happen to care for it. But I pray I'm wrong."

Not until many years later, when I repeated this line in front of an audience, did I learn that it was funny enough to get a laugh from a large group of strangers. And not just one time but many times before many different groups. Since then, much to my delight, I have discovered that my mother inadvertently authored a number of very reliable jokes, most of them at my expense. For example, on my thirtieth birthday I met my parents for dinner at a nice restaurant. My father ordered a bottle of champagne, and when it arrived, my mother proposed the following toast: "May half of all your dreams come true."

The table went silent.

"Mom," I said. "Isn't that kind of sad?"

"No," she immediately replied. "Half is a good percentage."

When I examine my own behavior, I can see that my lifelong compulsive desire to reinterpret every disagreeable and disparaging remark as funny can be traced back to my mother's gift for presenting so many things in a dispiriting light. She possessed a rare capacity to find something grim and problematic in even the happiest situation.

But in talking about her with others, I learned something interesting. Over the years, as I listened to my comedian friends discuss and dissect their childhoods, it gradually dawned on me that an awful lot of people who make a living in comedy owe their livelihoods to a similar kind of mom.

The comedian and novelist Bill Scheft likes to use the following quote when offering a thumbnail sketch of his mother: "You'll get unconditional love when you do something to deserve it." Then there's my friend George Meyer, comedy writer and for many years an important driving force behind *The Simpsons,* who describes his mother in an essay entitled "Gone, All Gone":

> Do you still have the adorable crayon drawings you
> made in kindergarten? I don't. Not a one. Which
> means that at one point, many years ago, the
> following thoughts must've gone through my
> mother's mind: "Hmm, what's this? Oh, I see. It's
> that irreplaceable drawing by my firstborn son. The
> one he proudly brought home from school. I'll just
> put this in the garbage." Then, as time went by:
> "Oh, another one of my child's drawings. What is it
> that I do with these again? Oh yes—I throw them

in the trash. That's right." Eventually her brain probably got it down to "Art—Son—Trash." And on days when my mom was sick, and didn't get around to throwing my artwork away, my dad would do it.

The beloved comedy icon Larry David, in an interview in the *L.A. Times* on June 18, 2009, spoke of his mother thusly: "The whole time I was doing *Seinfeld* she would call me up and she would go—and this is when the show was like . . . the number one show in the country—she would call me up, 'Do they like you, Larry? Do they think you're doing a good job? They must like you, otherwise they would fire you, wouldn't they? You wouldn't still be there if they didn't like you!'"

Larry David's remarks immediately reminded me of my mother's response years ago when I told her I was going to be having dinner with Peter Lassally, then one of the producers of *The Tonight Show.* "Well, if he invited you over for dinner, I guess he must like you," my mother said, as though I were presenting her with proof that the world is a miraculous place where wonders never cease.

I am not sure where these women got the idea that brutal honesty is an indispensable parenting tool, but Larry Amoros's mother apparently read the same manual. "When I was in fourth grade, we were having our class pictures taken," the comedian told me. "I asked my mother if I was handsome, and she said, matter-of-factly, 'No.' "

As painful as that probably was, I am here to point out the easily overlooked bright side. Larry Amoros's mother, like the other mothers, was teaching a valuable comedy lesson that dates back to the ancient Greeks: A casually cruel remark delivered in the face of innocent hopefulness is funny! Presumably because there is no other way to cope. When we laugh at a tactless remark, the world is happily returned to a place where outright rudeness can be seen for what it is: a betrayal of love and trust. Also: a fairly direct route to a laugh.

Which brings me to the positive contribution that Crazy Mommies have been making, unheralded, for generations. Yes, perhaps these are unconscious contributions, delivered at the cost of traumatic childhoods, but just as a half-full glass of milk is still a vitamin-rich glass of milk, a good standard-issue Crazy Mommy offers career nutrition by teaching her children that if they wish to retain their sanity, they had better start to see the awful things that happen to them as funny.

As Larry David also said (in that same *L. A. Times* story), "Positive is not funny. . . . When you speak in negative terms, the more negative, the funnier it is." And over time he has proved his point by including all the negative and uncomfortable things that ever happened anywhere near him in his work.

Of course, blindingly upbeat is also funny, as we see in the following piece of positive spin offered by George Meyer's mother, whom he quotes thusly: "Eileen Bleizig's husband just died. Which is fine. . . ." Still, Mr. David was correct that it is the perverse maternal attitude that most often creates children who are obsessed with being funny.

In fact, it recently occurred to me that these mothers might just be responsible for the existence of stand-up comedy as an art form. My research, if you can call it that,* shows that the lion's share† of compulsively funny people had a problematic relationship with a narcissistically inclined mother. The desire to rearrange grim facts into a joke seems to develop in direct proportion to the hysteria-filled humorlessness of the environment in which the Crazy‡ Mom in question conducted her family's daily affairs.

It's almost as though laughing at something horrible sets the clock back to a moment when everyone still had a normal level of optimism, logic, and mutual respect. Discovering a funny piece of terrain in an otherwise dreary landscape works like one of those doors that Bugs Bunny used to paint on a solid wall and then escape into anyway. Add a new and different perspective to a terrible moment, and an unexpected exit suddenly appears.

Yes, yes, I realize that the kind of problematic childhood I am describing can also produce children who kill small animals and/or average-sized members of the community, but for now let's focus on the disturbed people who become obsessed not with snuffing out the life force of strangers but with making assembled groups of them laugh (and, of course, later telling everyone how they "killed").

Comedy is, after all, about an imbalance of power. Therefore, creatively inclined children raised on the wrong side of a continuous power struggle end up developing an

---

*By "research," I am referring to the ridiculously high percentage of yeses I got when I asked my friends who pursue comedy for a living, "Did you have a crazy mom?"

†By "lion's share," I mean the African lion.

‡For "crazy," I'm using a very loose definition that encapsulates everything from clinical definitions of insanity to dinner-party anecdotes of unstable, inconsistent, or persistently exasperating motherly behavior.

ability to see the world as a setup in need of a punch line. At least a percentage of the smart ones know intuitively that it is a great way to make things appear, for a moment, sort of manageable.

For the creatively inclined, growing up under the thumb of a good old-fashioned insensitive, dismissive, difficult, or in some cases wholly unbalanced mommy can be a lot like growing up permanently enrolled in a graduate seminar in comedy. As she presents her child with an overwhelming set of unsolvable problems, while also promising and withholding her support, a Crazy Mommy instinctively inflicts just the right amount of emotional damage needed to provide her twitching offspring with the fortitude they will need to face down the drunken patrons of bars and nightclubs. Somehow, Crazy Mommy magically senses that by backing her kids into a corner, forcing them to feel alone and under attack in a world that doesn't make sense, she is also offering a hands-on daily workshop in how to assemble from scratch that most classic of all comedy characters: the disenfranchised, put-upon little guy.

And there's so much more! By doing her job correctly, every Crazy Mommy also provides her pulverized offspring with an essential starter pack of unfortunate situations on which they can base their first original jokes.

The comedian Cory Kahaney offers the following example: "So my sister just started therapy, and I am very supportive because I am in therapy for fourteen years. Not that I have the greatest therapist—it's just the longest relationship I ever had. Anyway, I tell my sister, 'That's great you're in therapy,' and she says, 'Yeah, but I think I should let you know I confronted Mommy about the "lunches."' And I am like, 'The "lunches"? What "lunches"?' And she says, 'You know, the fact that she never made our lunch.' So I said, 'Oh yeah, the lunches. See, I would've started with the beatings.'"

In some cases, daily life with Crazy Mommy is like watching an endless one-woman show in which she stars as the poor beleaguered keeper of the flame, suffering at the hands of tyrannical children. Since she alone seems to be in charge of the whole production, she leaves her kids no choice but to set about trying to rewrite their own parts. Depending on how well they are able to do this, they can begin to imagine they are in an entirely different play.

"How to describe the family Amoros?" says comedian Larry Amoros. "Imagine *Grey Gardens,* but without Jackie Kennedy. My mother told me that I had an older brother named Melvin, who attended a boarding school for very smart children, which is why I'd never met him. But if he died, then I could be the smart one. When I was fourteen my father became ill, and anytime I'd do anything horrifically, egregiously wrong (like chew with my mouth open or drop a napkin), my mother would yell, 'That's right, upset your father. Put him in the ground.'"

When inevitably the day comes that the child grows up and has metamorphosed into a rage-filled comedian, standing alone in a darkened room full of Crazy Mommy substitutes who have now paid money for the privilege of offering their conditional love as audience members (which completes the circle by including the right to scream mean things at the person they are watching on the stage), he or she will also know intuitively how to maintain his or her cool under pressure, thanks to all those years of practice deflecting Crazy Mommy.

Don't forget that although the world at large may roll their eyes as each Crazy Mommy goes on her appointed rounds, the children she raises are required to take her seriously as long as they live in her home. They are told to accept her point of view as reasonable, and to obey it without question. And this they are expected to continue indefinitely into adulthood if they want familial peace, as we see in this cautionary tale from the comedian Wendy Liebman: "The day before my first/only wedding at age forty-two, I said to my mother, 'Mommy, please don't play the drums tomorrow.' Yes, I still call her 'Mommy.' I told her not to play the drums because she loves to play the drums and has been known to sit in with the band at functions where there is a band. She says, 'Why not?' I say, 'Well, it's my only wedding, and I just don't want you to play the drums.' 'Okay,' she says. Cut to the night of the wedding, after she's had some wine: I see her make a beeline for the drums. I step into her path and look her in the face. 'Mommy, what are you doing?' I say. She says, without missing a beat, no pun intended, 'I'm going to play the drums.' I stand there speechless. My new husband of three hours looks at me and says, 'Let her play the drums.' My mother played the drums at my wedding."

So we see that a standard model Crazy Mommy, with her inability to see her children as separate human beings who have their own easily bruised feelings, is also supplying them with all the important paving stones on the path to becoming funny. The comedian and writer April Winchell also offered an example from her childhood of both skewed maternal judgment and the comedic usefulness of a carefully placed non sequitur: "There was a local TV show on when I was a kid called *The Sandy Becker Show*. He had kids on and talked to them. So when my sister was about eight she wanted to be on it more than anything. My father pulled a few strings and got her on the show. While she was backstage, a couple of wardrobe mistresses got into a nasty argument, and one of them called the other one a 'dyke.' My sister went to my mother and asked her what a dyke was, and my mother said, 'She's a woman who never gets married,' which wasn't too bad for 1958. Finally, it was my sister's turn to go out onstage and talk to Sandy Becker. She went out and sat on his lap. He started asking her questions: What do you like to do? What do you want to be when you grow up? Finally he asked her if she wanted to get married, and she said, 'Oh no, I'm going to be a dyke.' After that, they hustled her off the stage pretty quick. She was devastated; she had no idea what happened. Sobbing, she asked my mother why they took her off the show. And do you know what my mother said? 'Your head was too big to fit on the screen.'"

I grant you that at first glance the very idea of a childhood so hammered by insensitive behavior that it creates people driven to seek love and attention from inebriated strangers may seem truly pathetic. But it's also lovely that show business exists to provide this kind of arena, where the emotionally pummeled can offer their wounds for the inebriated to lick.

Perhaps the most ironic part of the whole Crazy Mommy syndrome is that even after the comedian in training has grown up, moved away from home, and bothered to achieve enough status in show business to offer his or her discounting parent concrete evidence of his or her success in the outside world, it rarely changes the original parent-child dynamic. Our friend Bill Scheft discovered this when he took pains to alert his mother that he was going to be on the radio. After his appearance, he asked her if she had enjoyed the show. "I heard the beginning," she said, "but then you started talking about people I didn't know, so I turned it off."

Bill's wife, the comedian Adrianne Tolsch, tells of the time when she found out that she was going to be in *Newsweek* magazine in a big article featuring her as one of the new "Queens of Comedy." "I called Mom, dizzyingly excited and proud. 'Mom, *Newsweek* magazine called me one of the new queens of comedy!' I said. 'A two-page spread, with a picture and everything!!' . . . And Mom said, 'You don't say hello? You don't say how are you? And we don't get that magazine here.' She lived in Los Angeles."

Then there's the comedian friend (who asked to remain anonymous) who tells the story of coming home for the holidays right after she had broken up with her comedian boyfriend. "My father would *not* stop praising him. I finally said, 'How can you be so enamored with a man who didn't love your daughter?' This made my father so angry, he stormed away from the dinner table. At that point, my mother stared daggers at me and said, 'I can't believe you. Your father has never known anyone who was on *The Tonight Show* before.' "

It's in our DNA to believe that our mothers have our best interests at heart. The idea is presented as truth in every corner of our culture. Clearly there's a wide assortment of ways to define "best interests." I even wrote this essay in order to try to recast otherwise disturbing anecdotes into something useful and uplifting. Because no matter how uncomfortable the circumstances were the first time through, it's a really gratifying gift when an audience laughs at an awful narrative from a painful past. It's almost like some kind of heavenly jury has redecided an unfair original verdict in favor of the poor weary kid with the saner perspective.

Therefore, when people ask me, as they sometimes do, how to get into comedy, I have mainly one piece of advice. I tell them, try to be raised by a woman who has at least five or six of the following traits, which I culled from descriptive lists solicited from the people whose Crazy Mommy stories you just read: bright, clever, crafty, fearless, complex, artistic, resourceful, and inventive *while at the same time* oblivious, controlling, manipulative, neurotic, tasteless, intractable, solipsistic, thwarted, repressed, inconsistent, critical, self-destructive, depressed, angst-ridden, furious, suicidal, violent, narcissistic, fearful, self-loathing, selfish, and sadistic.

If your mother has some qualities from each of the two areas, congratulations. Entertainment-starved drunks await you!

Naturally, the legacy of a mother like this is not only upbeat. Side effects may also include the inability to ever trust anyone or feel at ease with yourself. You may also experience depression, hypersensitivity, obsessive compulsive disorder, masochism, backaches, migraines, rashes, eating disorders, and other rage-related symptoms. In my own case, my mother's relentless micromanagement and harsh criticism instilled in me a sense of insecurity that, some twenty years after her death, can be managed but not eradicated entirely. And I got off easy. Dealing with my mother was not nearly as difficult as it must have been for my comedian friends who tell stories about alcoholic, drug-addicted, manic-depressive, narcissistic, sadistic, and Munchausen by proxy mommies.

Fortunately, we live in an era where therapy and counseling lurk around every corner. Especially in Los Angeles and New York, where a lot of comedians wind up. Comedians are to the therapy economy what ten-year-old boys are to the videogame industry.

Because I had been seeing a therapist for three or four years, when my mother insisted that I show her a television show that I had written and also appeared in, I decided to try out a new approach in my ongoing effort to make our interactions less painful. So after agreeing to let her watch a video of my work, I presented her with a condition. "It's too late now to change anything," I said to her. "I'd like to request a favor: No matter how you feel about what you see, just lie and say, 'Hey! Nice job!' and leave it at that!" I smiled and showed her how to give me a thumbs-up and a big delighted grin.

In response, my mother stared at me, her features frozen in an unsmiling mask. "If I can't criticize you, what are we supposed to talk about? The weather?" she finally said.

Never Again

Sometimes I like to imagine myself flying over a map of my life on Google Earth. I know just what it would look like, too. There, rising out of the ocean, beyond those burned-out campfire pits along the rocky coast of Northern California, are the precipitous cliffs of my teenage years. I zoom past those quickly, scrolling, scrolling, making sure I don't get trapped on some craggy ledge where I'll be stuck staring down at my tenth-grade yearbook photo. God, I hate my hair like that.

Instead, I head farther north, riding over the forests and parklands of the Sierras until, on the horizon, I spot the volcano that was my twenties. Once a sputtering, lava-erupting embodiment of a million noisy unsolvable problems, now it looks placid and quaint, no hint of the bedlam it intended to spew onto the nearby townspeople.

From there I glide south toward the desert, soaring and circling like a hawk on a thermal, enjoying the vast expanses of barren terrain full of rocks and boulders. I float out over some eerie sandstone spires at the edge of a dilapidated ghost town until I spot the boarded-up entrance to an abandoned mine. That was my thirties, now covered with cobwebs and crawling with scorpions. No good reason to spend much time here, either.

So I head east, then continue in a northerly direction, enjoying the tidy geometry of nicely tended farmland until a burned-out, pockmarked area is looming before me. The contrast in topography is so stark that for a second it makes me gasp. I'm looking down on a massive, rutted field full of rusted barbed wire, shallow graves, and muddy zigzagging dugouts that resemble the trenches of the Battle of Verdun. Too high up to see the gory details, I keep clicking on the map to enlarge it until scavenging rats and feral cats come into focus. Now I can also make out all kinds of familiar-looking things mixed up in this wet toxic sludge: ticket stubs from sports events I pretended to be watching, half-full bottles of men's toiletries that were left behind after the first grenade was launched. The closer I get, the more I can spot other familiar fragments: grimy disintegrated letters containing adorable nicknames too humiliating to acknowledge; torn pieces of playfully staged photos from assorted decades. Those clowning, grinning, muggy faces and poses certainly looked a lot more winsome at the time. Where am I? What is this icky place?

Surprise: I am hovering over the grizzled terrain of my love life, starting at age eighteen.

Ah, love. What a pain in the ass it has been since I met it.

That feeling of obsession and elation resulting from an intense moment of chemistry with a member of the opposite sex I barely knew but felt close to because we'd gone out for coffee... followed by the anxiety, the turmoil, the misunderstandings and inappropriate expectations that come from being thrust into a state of intimacy with a complete stranger.

In my checkered past, I have had four long-term (as in more than three years) "love" relationships, all vying for the title of goofiest or most delusional. So glaring were their shortcomings that at no point did I seriously consider marriage, for fear of turning the sacred vow of "forever" into a sarcastic remark. But having a clear picture of the limitations of these liaisons did not keep me from moving in with these men and sticking around for a long time. That's because in my youth, living with a nutty, unreliable guy made the same good common sense as having sex on the first date. As far as I was concerned, it was unreasonable to think of forgoing fun solely on the grounds that it might be counterproductive. After all, incomprehensible, spontaneous chaos was the first real step on the path to having the deeper, richer "life experiences" required for making good art.

By the time the last of these relationships ended I was such a quaking mass of colliding, exploding neurotransmitter malfunctions that the only coherent sentence I could form in my native tongue went: "Never again."

So there I was, trapped in that damp, mildew-covered portal between the eighties and the nineties, obsessively analyzing memories of ancient conversations with old boyfriends in search of some hidden second layer of meaning that wouldn't become visible for many years.

Ah, the eighties.

Who didn't love those happy-go-lucky days when single women could luxuriate in a delightful study that claimed that the chances of a woman in her forties being killed by a terrorist were greater than her chances of getting married? In retrospect, the only remotely beneficial by-product of 9/11 was the instant and radical change in the terrorist murder/ marriage odds in favor of older single women.

Then again, what were we expecting? If someone had told Mother Nature at the dawn of creation that there would come a day when her sons and daughters would be doing Jell-O shots and going to Ozzfest in their forties, fifties, and sixties, sometimes still in hopes of hooking up with their ultimate soul mates . . . she would have laughed derisively. Then, if she was feeling irritable, she would have made the whole species extinct.

Unless I'm misunderstanding something, Mother Nature's Original Plan for the Dating and Mating of All Creatures was basically this: when said creatures were in their teens, they were supposed to attract the healthiest, most genetically desirable members of their own species and procreate. They were meant to do it pretty quickly, too, judging by the time span between meeting and mating allowed for in nearly every other life-form, which can usually be measured in hours, if not minutes or seconds.

And once the act of giving birth was over, all bets were off. There's very little evidence that Mother Nature saw happiness as the next logical step for the new family. In fact, she seems to be fine with cannibalism (sharks, hamsters, and chimps all eat their young), fratricide (when black eagles have two chicks, the stronger one kills the weaker one), infanticide (monkeys, ducks, and pigs keep the size of their broods down by killing the extras), and child abandonment (pandas let all but one cub die; black bears walk away from their babies unless there are at least three).

But that's for *those guys*. We humans like to rewrite and improve Mother Nature's rules wherever possible. Thus we have reinterpreted a successful postcoital union to mean one in which both parties are giddy with love day and night, forever, until they die. (Or until the end of time, whichever comes first.) If things get Grumpy or Sleepy or Dopey (or any of the seven dwarfs except Happy), a Greek chorus of empathetic friends and relatives of the dissatisfied couple— most of whom are several times divorced—steps forward from the shadows to helpfully chant, "You're too good for this. Leave." That's because American humans now live in the Age of Perpetual High School. It's the first time in human history in which two-thirds of the over-eighteen population feel that they do not yet have the credits they need to matriculate to adulthood. Twenty has become an extension of the teens, thirty is "postadolescent," and forty is "still a kid getting started."

When my last relationship ended, and I was just a kid starting out, about to turn forty, I was as eager to begin to search for another perfect soul mate as I was to volunteer for hard labor in a North Korean prison camp. The world seemed to be broken down into two factions: those who were twitching from horrible divorces and those who were still pretending to be seventeen.

On the rare occasions when I would send a periscope up to survey the possibilities around the edges of the dating pool, no one looked as tanned and glowing as they did the last time I had checked.

So there we all were, sallow, grouchy, sunburned survivors of a million rancid romantic entanglements, shivering in the shallow end of the pool and pissed off that I was using swimming pool metaphors because it meant we all had to look at each other in swimwear. Even worse was the realization that our only choices were forcing ourselves to date again or total abstinence.

And now that we'd reached this crossroads, the only thing the bunch of us had in common was our very specific egocentrically derived lists of the things we could no longer tolerate.

Obviously, a lot of the older males had decided they preferred younger women. Their motivation needed no explanation not covered by the word "duh." There was also a less obvious second reason that these geezers sought out the youngsters. Young women, bless their little pinheads, manage to convince themselves that once the word "Love" is in play, they can single-handedly fix any problems that may arise by making a few simple hair and wardrobe adjustments. Only women under twenty-five believe that working your way through a women's magazine's list of "102 new things that he says turn him on" will affect anything except that magazine's advertising rates.

Older women, even by their mid-thirties, have their own strategies for eliminating candidates. Many have been to therapy, read a few self-help books, or watched a lot of *Oprah*. Thus they stare grim-faced, eyes rolling, when confronting men their own age who are trying to recycle the antique repertoire of vintage relationship bullshit they got away with in their twenties. The counterarguments these men like (for example, "How was I supposed to know?" or "I don't get why that is such a big deal") sound a lot more pathetic coming from a dude who looks like someone's corny father.

"You've got to be kidding me" is not the response these men want to hear.

In my own case, by the time I was attempting resocialization, I had consumed and digested so much therapeutic advice via shrinks, books, radio, television, and the Internet that I couldn't lay eyes on a new man without making a mental catalogue of his flaws. Halfway through his first sentence, I would have him filed by psychological and emotional dysfunction. I would have decided whether he was a primary or secondary narcissist or sociopath, a substance abuser, a depressive, bipolar, an obsessive-compulsive, a hysteric, a neurotic, or a delightful combination of them all. I would also be looking for the iceberg tips of dangerous issues lurking in his mannerisms, his facial expressions, his vocal inflections, and the contents of his refrigerator.

So specific and extensive was my checklist of human frailty that for the next twelve years I shared my home only with a large herd of dogs and their tumbleweed-sized wads of floating hair. It was lonely, but not all *that* lonely. My dogs were enthusiastic supporters of everything I did. They not only overlooked my flaws, they embraced and celebrated them. My weakest, most halfhearted attempts at cooking were greeted as though they were culinary achievements. When I was too lazy to shower, they liked that better than when I dressed up.

I began to see myself as their alpha, a canine-pack-dwelling Jane Goodall (minus all the tedious research and charity work). And in those years of solitude and contemplation, I tried to pursue a regimen of peace, maturity, and self-esteem (by which I mean attempting to limit myself to two despondent statements per day about "not having a life").

Eventually, though, I hit critical mass and had to admit that I really *did* want to be a part of another tiny unit of humans, even if it meant setting myself up for a possible emotional slaughter. I'm not sure what constituted the last straw. It may have been sheer exhaustion from trying to talk the other single women I knew into clearing spaces in their busy schedules in order to attend things meant to get me out of the house. Or maybe it was the way the dogs just kept snoring through my pleas for help with bringing stuff in from the car.

Either way, my edict of "Never again" gradually morphed into "Never again unless I get married." My thinking was that if I could take that additional step toward greater permanence, a step that had always eluded me, I would undergo an almost mystical transformation from confused member of the minority of loners and weirdos into the safer territory of the majority, with their holy matrimony, lawsuits, divorces, and mutual restraining orders.

Someplace in the middle of my confusion about what step I needed to take next, and long after I had given up entirely, I attended a theatrical event where I met a man who seemed funny and smart. We began exchanging quippy emails. Because this guy was in a happy relationship at the time, the emails weren't flirtatious, just entertaining, especially after they escalated into a storytelling contest to see who could rightfully claim the title of the all-time biggest idiot in the name of love. I began the contest knowing I would win, but became alarmed when I realized that his stories were turning out to be a lot more dire and catastrophe-filled than mine. Still, I knew I would triumph anyway, because I planned to claim to have been an accomplice to a homicidal crime of passion. Why not? This guy didn't know me. He didn't know my history. How could he prove me wrong?

Fortunately, the contest ended before I had to transform old plots from *CSI: Miami* into convincing personal anecdotes. By then I had begun to realize that our emails had become the only coherent nuanced conversation I was having with a two-legged polysyllabic creature on a regular basis. They were a reminder that I, as a human being, had a need to communicate in ways more layered and complex than simple ball throwing.

Therefore, when his girlfriend left and he became single, I had no hesitation about dating this guy. And when I say "date," I mean wake up at two in the morning to accommodate his late-night schedule as a musician. His workday started when I was finishing dinner.

"No, no, three A.M. isn't too late for a visit," I would lie as I searched my cabinets for a box of Vivarin. Then, having consumed in pill form the equivalent of ten cups of coffee, I would shower, put on makeup, and whip up a little entrée I hoped he would find half as impressive as the dogs found my mostly empty salad bowls. Spending a decade alone, as it turns out, makes a person more amenable to the idea of thin-slicing mushrooms for chicken marsala at three in the morning.

After so many years of isolation, I kind of enjoyed the late-night activity. I began to realize that there were advantages to older love. For instance, by the time this guy met me,

I could actually cook something more complicated than oatmeal.

Once things between us started percolating, I found that stepping into the relationship arena at the cusp of (some age or other) was quite a different experience than it had been in previous decades. Younger love, it seemed, was mainly about the idea of potential—the illusion that magical transformations were bound to occur when the person you think you love has a miraculous unprompted awakening after some metaphorical lightning bolt, made out of your wishes and projections, suddenly brings them to their senses. On the other hand, older love is all about what you are hoping is still possible, after you have mourned the death of the idea of yourself as a manufacturer of miracles. Older love starts with the unpleasant truth that expecting a person to change for the better spontaneously, simply because you wish it, makes as much sense as counting on the lottery for next month's rent.

My new gentleman caller stood out immediately from his predecessors. For one thing, since we weren't living together, he didn't have the option of yelling "Okay, then get the fuck out!" when tempers flared. This meant that even irrational fights eventually ended with a discussion containing adult perspective, introspection, and resolution, a marked improvement over olden times, when I seemed to always be the one to shrug before retreating to my bunker to silently embrace the rashes, stomachaches, and asthma attacks that accompanied unilateral disarmament.

Now, after many years of therapy, I had learned how to stand my ground. No more volunteering that everything was my fault, especially on those occasions when everything actually *was* my fault.

And so it came to pass that almost three years into a relationship where we saw each other only on weekends and Wednesdays, my gentleman friend called me to say that his landlord had decided to sell the house he was renting and now he was going to have to look for a place to live. No one was more surprised than I to hear my mouth speaking the words "Well, then, why don't you move in with me?"

While I spoke, I could feel my stomach knot as I was swallowed up in a rapid montage of fiery images from the dying moments of previous relationships: the lying, the swearing, the screaming, the vitriol, the day I filled a car with a boyfriend's clothes as if it were some engine-driven suitcase and had it removed from the premises. "I hope you know what you're doing," I said to myself, "because I am not sure I was properly consulted on this decision."

Cut to: one bright summer day, as I was helping this new man pack his belongings into cardboard boxes from Staples.

"What about your edict?" I asked myself, aware that I was ignoring it the same way I do my New Year's resolutions. "Remember that thing you said about never living with another man unless you got married first?"

"Well, I'm not sure I ever said *that,*" I replied, as I rifled through his cupboards, throwing away the pots I'd seen cats sleeping in. "You know me. I'm always making jokes. I can't keep track of everything I say!"

"No, you definitely said it," I argued. "You were acting like it was a big revelation. I think if you consult your diaries you will find that you wrote it down."

"Do you have any idea how many diaries I have?" I sighed, opening and closing closets, checking to see if there was anything useful inside we needed to pack.

"You won't have to go through all of them, because I can put a date on when you said it," I reminded myself helpfully, even as I was tuning myself out and heading outside to help pile boxes into the back of my car so we could get to the post office and file a forwarding address before it closed for the day. "Why did you ever say 'Never again unless I get married' if you were going to totally ignore it?"

"Well, I've only known him for three years," I argued back. "Don't you think it's a little premature?"

"Plus two years of emailing," I argued right back. "That's five years."

"Five years in the context of a human life is not that long. Have you ever met a five-year-old child? They are basically infants. Tiny babies," I said.

"Getting married is an important thing. Gay couples wake up feeling like second-class citizens for being denied the opportunity to do what you're avoiding," I replied, shaking my head in disgust.

"Well, then why does everybody end up getting divorced and saying they will never get married again?" I countered as I drove his stuff across town.

"For the same reason that you said you would never live with someone again without being married," I explained. "Will you stand still for a minute? I am getting sick of following you from one room to the next!"

"Listen to me," I said. "Why do you have to make such a big deal out of everything?"

"I make a big deal out of this because it *is* a big deal, or else why is this whole country in a contentious debate trying to keep gay people out of the marriage club?"

"You're just being a contrarian," I replied. "Marriage is one more thing you refuse to play along with because it is expected of you, like being on Facebook. Admit it: you just delay final decisions on everything because you're wishy-washy."

"If you're going to start calling me names, then this discussion is over," I said as I was going through the big display case in my front room, throwing out my snow globes to make space for his ceramic Napoleons. Then I stalked out and never bothered to talk to myself about this again.

Back to my flight over that Google Earth map of my life.

Now when I'm airborne and gliding above those worrisome corpse-strewn trenches of Verdun that gape like surface wounds after an asteroid collision, I quickly head due west, then north, where I come to a recent addition: an improved recreation area full of rolling hills, a manicured picnic area, and a lake surrounded by flowering trees. It seems to make the rest of the map look more balanced, less haunted and disturbing—visual proof that there is a payoff for having had a checkered past. How nice to see that at some point, you find that you've gotten better at checkers.

So where edicts are concerned: never again.

Why I Love Dogs

I LOVE DAVID ATTENBOROUGH DOCUMENTARIES. I WATCH THEM over and over. Every three-toed sloth hanging on the underside of a tree branch and every grimacing hyena that walks in slow motion across a grassy plain fills me with empathy and awe. I immediately begin to yearn for quality time with blue-footed boobies, proboscis monkeys, and frill-necked lizards. I want to be close to them, to help them forage for potato bugs, or dung beetles, or whatever it is they have in mind for dinner. That is because the idea of living with a member of another species has always seemed enlightening as well as thrilling.

No wonder I fell in love with dogs from the moment I met any of them and found out how willing they were to share my home.

From my earliest experiences, dogs have not really been pets to me so much as exceedingly cooperative exchange students from another planet. In our unlikely union, mystified though we are by each other's habits and customs, I continue to be impressed by how they are willing to meet me halfway. In most cases, not only are they eager to cooperate, they are fine with doing it on my terms at the location and time of day of my choosing! (Well, maybe not with the things they find patently insane. For example: waiting until sunrise for meals.)

I got my first dog when I was in kindergarten and instantly found his presence to be comforting and entertaining. After a long day of dealing with teachers and parents who seemed impossible to please, what a relief it was to join, in progress, a species who honestly felt at any given moment, that "this is the best moment of my life... Until right now, which is slightly better... Wait, I meant *this*... No, *this*... No, I spoke too soon. This moment right *now* is the best one ever."

And if we hit a lull or a snag, all that was required to set everything back to perfect again was a cookie, a simple item whose massive importance has no real equivalent in the restless, fickle world of the human.

But along with the ability to value life's simple things, if I'm being completely honest, I would also have to admit that dogs err on the side of being a teensy bit self-absorbed. Though I must add that of the fifteen dogs with whom I have shared my home since childhood, not a single one has ever let me down—providing I adjusted my expectations so that they were in line with what the dogs had in mind to deliver anyway. Thus it's also hard not to conclude that in some ways dogs may be the biggest narcissists of all.

After many years of therapy, I can't really tolerate human narcissists anymore. I don't care about their tragic self-doubts or the roots of their pain and rage. Yet oddly enough, I still love being around dogs. When I try to analyze why, it's definitely hard to figure. It certainly isn't because of the behaviors they exhibit around me, which, taken at face value, are pretty disturbing.

For instance, if even the most adorable man or beloved family member insisted on busting in through the bathroom door and running up to kiss me every time I sat down on the toilet—not just once or twice but *every single time* I went to the bathroom—then stood around staring adoringly, mesmerized by my activities, not only would I find it unnerving, it would fill me with fury. If the person were a relative, this scenario would become an unending topic with the shrink. If it were my husband, it might be grounds for divorce.

I also wouldn't find it cute or in any way entertaining to have an assortment of my seemingly inconsolable friends hovering behind me while I was cooking: rushing in to lick any spills or crumbs up off the floor, than staring, drooling, and pleading with me to give them a morsel of food. Even if they had earned my empathy with their stories of escape from some violent, war-torn homeland, I would still find this blatant bit of manipulation so offensive that I would turn and, in a harsh tone of voice, insist that each of them leave the room.

But if, after I did this, they only went as far as the door and then stood there continuing to stare at me and make sorrowful pouty faces, it is unlikely that I would reinforce them further by relenting and giving each of them a small bowl of whatever I was preparing, followed by a kiss on the head. And if, for some reason, I did do this, and their follow-up reaction was to gulp whatever I'd given them down in a single swallow, then look up at me with streams of whatever it was dripping off their noses and chins while still continuing to try to gain my sympathy by appearing wretched, I can guarantee you that I would not react by saying "Awww" and asking them if they might like another helping.

The wide berth I cut for dogs runs counter to the way I have learned, over time, to deal with the dilemma of terrible houseguests. Throughout my life, I have had a number of unfortunate incidents with people who have abused my hospitality by alienating me with their inconsiderate behavior. I have deplored their incompatible rising times, their complaints about the menu, their impulse to talk while I was working. When their stay was over, I was always gleeful as they departed, vowing never to let them spend the night again.

Which is why it is hard to imagine inviting not just one person but four to stay with me for fifteen years, aware that they not only do not speak my language but will never make the slightest attempt to learn. Plus they will also expect me to pay all their medical bills and funeral expenses: privileges I, of course, happily offer my dogs. How insufferable would it be if even one person who came to stay exhibited so little interest in my daily affairs that they never so much as asked what I did for a living? How rude would it seem if they never even offered to help with the dishes? It would not be the least bit endearing if, say, my brother and his family jumped on top of me in the morning before I woke up, then stood there looming over me at six A.M. yelling, "Food! Food! Food! Food!" And if I tried to ignore them by rolling onto my side and placing a pillow over my head and they proceeded to put their faces right next to mine and make whimpering noises, I doubt that my reaction would be to compliment them on their intuitive timekeeping abilities, then jump up, give them a hug, and make them breakfast. Not only that, but also happily pick up all the toys and clothes and garbage they had knocked onto the floor and shredded, no questions asked.

And after breakfast, I definitely wouldn't allow them to sit with me in my office for hours on end, staring at me while I worked on a book.

If, say, my grandmother sat on my feet, under my desk, her face visible somewhere down by my knees, and every now and then reached over to scratch me on my calf with her really sharp nails before unexpectedly letting out a loud wail of agony that had no meaning except as a way to remind me that there was some activity she wanted me to share with her, well, I can tell you right now that I would want to spend *less* time with Grandma, not more. I not only wouldn't be moved to comfort her, I also cannot imagine remarking about how clever she was, then agreeing to go out with her for a walk. More likely I would mutter something harsh about needing time to myself, just before ordering her to take her damn walks alone.

In fact, a grandmother who behaved like this would be so on my last nerve that after I got up and moved into the other room with my laptop, if she followed me and came over and sat right on top of my keyboard, knocking off all my papers and books, and tried to kiss me, I would scream and tell her to get the fuck out of here right now. And then if a little later I found her sprawled out in the middle of the hallway in front of the door to my bedroom, oblivious to the fact that because she was using up all the available floor space I was having to jump over her just to get into my own room, my reaction would not be "Awwww, see how much she trusts me?" I would be so insanely aggrieved that I would stop speaking to that grandmother entirely. Then when I got the time, I would change my email address and my phone number.

Because the truth is, I cannot imagine continuing to love anyone who had the gall to think that it was acceptable, after many hours spent digging in the mud, to crawl into my bed, lean up against me like a fifty-pound sack of rice, and make snoring noises like a broken exhaust pipe. In fact, I have never thought the sleeping position of any man I loved deeply, even if we were spooning after a passionate encounter, was so adorable that I wouldn't wake him up and ask him to move when I felt my arms going numb.

It's also not likely that I would be motivated to maintain a cordial long-term relationship with any human being, no matter how attractive or influential, who emitted sulfurous odors every time they sat down beside me. I would be correct to find this behavior unspeakably boorish, and sensible to resent having to interrupt my activities while the room was airing out.

It's too unpleasant to even fantasize about what would happen if the man I lived with behaved that way among people I cared about during a dinner party, to say nothing of putting his head down on the table right next to the full plate of one of my guests, in the hopes that she would hand over some of her food. Oh sure, I guess at first I would try to ban him from the room. But if he refused to go, then ran under the table and started to weep, and I later discovered that he had stolen all the extra food off the counter in the kitchen and taken it out into the yard, where he had eaten it behind a row of shrubs, leaving behind big wads of partially eaten

Saran Wrap and aluminum foil, what recourse would I have but to accuse him of having an untreated mental illness and, after the guests went home, insist that he seek professional treatment? I would get a restraining order to keep him off the premises. And if that didn't work, I would sell my house and move.

And if all of these things continued to happen, plus I found that he kept taking dirty napkins out of the trash and shredding them in order to extract all the last remaining food particles before scattering them all over the rugs ... or standing directly in front of the TV screen, right in the middle of the inauguration of the first black president of the United States of America, happily squeaking on a noisemaker for no reason ... what choice would I have but to suspect that this person had sadistic motives and a dangerous emotional disorder?

So it must be something else my dogs are doing that makes me love them so much.

Because there's no way in the world that I would consciously want any part of living with anyone who exhibited these types of behaviors.

But Enough About Me: Narcissism for Echoes*

EVERY YEAR, AT CHRISTMAS, MY MOTHER WOULD BUY ME AN expensive piece of clothing that I would never wear. Or, if luck was smiling on me, several pieces of expensive clothing meant to be worn together that I would never wear. I describe the clothing as "expensive" because when my mother gave me these gifts, she would make a point of telling me how much each piece cost. Not only that, she would also detail how much effort she had put into traipsing through stores, braving ungodly crowds of holiday shoppers in order to score this rare and superior-quality item for me.

"You need to be especially careful with this one," she

---

*A few years ago I was asked to write about "a valuable life lesson." This layman's explanation of narcissism was the result. Upon publication, I got so many responses from people who, like myself, had been previously puzzled, saying, "Thanks. I was *wondering* what that was!" that I have included it here, in the name of being helpful.

would say, as I unwrapped the box. "That's a hundred and thirty-five dollars' worth of mohair."

"Wow, it's beautiful!" I would exclaim, trying my hardest to cover any honest emotion that might be sliding onto my face. Because the most difficult part of this ritual was that every year, without fail, my mother would miss the mark of my taste by such a wide margin that I thought she might know an alternate universe version of me who dressed in ethnic print skirts with gathered waists and blouses with Peter Pan collars festooned with appliqué ducks holding umbrellas.

I began to dread her gifts because from December 26 on they hung in my closet unworn, glaring and fuming, causing me shame for having squandered my mother's time and money. There was also the looming fear that she would find a reason to go poking around in my closet someday and discover that all the clothes she had bought for me looked too pressed and untouched by the elements to have ever been worn.

Of course, the holidays always allowed our fraught relationship to blossom into a full-blown drama, courtesy of the potent combination of leisure time and forced festivity. But no such special occasion was needed for my mother and me to fill our time together with tension.

"These can't be the only knives you have?" my mother might say on any visit, her irritation and disbelief joining forces to create the tone of voice I carried around in my head to berate myself with at all times. She had programmed me well. I knew instinctively what she would dislike, but that didn't mean I could necessarily correct all her areas of complaint before her arrival. It was easier to predict what she wouldn't like than to guess what she would.

So I was resigned to coping with every Christmas in as genial and low-key a way as possible. Then I had an idea.

It came to me in the middle of the night as I lay awake, a thirty-five-year-old woman fretting about what would happen if she didn't get all-new place settings before dinner on D-day.

The following morning I phoned my mother and suggested that we try shopping for my Christmas gift *together*. I didn't expect her to go for it. I was thrilled when she agreed.

Best of all, I already knew what I wanted: a black fitted blazer that I could wear with everything—a noncontroversial selection that couldn't get shot down as a "ridiculous choice." It would be stylish, versatile, and just expensive enough for my mother to be able to boast about how much she had spent on it. It would herald the end to my guilt about unworn presents. My mother would buy me something that I actually wanted! What an exhilarating idea!

On the appointed day, my mother and I walked around crowded department stores for hours on end as she waved hangers full of ethnic print skirts with gathered waists and blouses with Peter Pan collars at me as though she were some kind of naval officer on the brig, signaling to the rest of the team on the shore. Reluctant to fire the first shot, I made sure to smile and say, "Yes! Lovely!" or "Wow!!! Beautiful!" as she displayed each new ensemble.

But I stood my ground.

After dozens of inappropriate selections from my mother, I held up an example of what I had come here to find. "I could really use a new black blazer...like this!" I said, trying to seem jaunty and casual. My mother made one of her patented grim faces. Hers was the expression of a displeased banker in a Charles Dickens adaptation, accompanied by a curled-lip "yecccch" as she insisted that I at least try on the clothes she'd picked out first.

I played along, thinking to myself, as I viewed her selections, that if my goal was to look fifteen years older and thirty pounds heavier, these were definitely the outfits I would choose.

At the end of the day, as closing time was requiring us to wrap this party up, I took a deep breath and said, "Mom, as much as I love all those things you showed me, I really need a new black blazer for work." I saw her sigh deeply. "It's the perfect gift for me right now," I went on. "I'll look capable and no-nonsense but feminine at the same time. I can wear it to a meeting or dinner or on the rifle range, you know . . . if I ever have a reason to go to a rifle range. Or a dinner."

My mother rolled her eyes and exhaled such an exasperated gust of air that it almost caused all the clothing on the racks in the women's sportswear department to sway. Then she muttered bitterly, as she handed her Visa card to the cashier, "This is the last time I am doing anything like this. I get no pleasure from buying you something I don't happen to like."

A few minutes later, as I followed her out of the store, carrying my "present" in a garment bag, she could barely look at me. Somehow I had gone and done it again: ruined Christmas for my mother.

How had it all gone so horribly wrong?

Some of the most valuable lessons I've learned in life are the small ones. For example, someone once told me, "When you have your picture taken, smile. If it turns out to be a bad picture, at least you don't also look like an asshole."

And then there are big complex lessons. Comprehending the mechanism of the narcissistic personality was one of those for me.

The subject was brought to my attention after I made an appointment to see a shrink, seeking, among other things, an explanation of the aforementioned Christmas mystery, which was really just one of many bafflingly similar incidents that had cluttered my life for years. I had begun to notice that my parents and boyfriends had similar complaints about me. For example, the boyfriend I had at that time would become enraged if I stayed up to watch a movie by myself instead of going to bed at the same time he did, whether or not I was sleepy. He felt that my actions, unconcerned as they were with bearing witness to the innate majesty of his slumber, proved that I cared only about myself. "Why does everything always have to be done *your* way?" he railed.

This puzzled me because it didn't sound like what was going on from my perspective. Staying up late didn't feel like an act of teenage rebellion. I wasn't refusing to follow orders because I was competing with him for the title of sleep captain. I was only staying up because I knew that something boring on television would eventually put my brain to sleep. Few things in life could be predicted with more certainty.

There had to be, I said to myself, something I was missing. It couldn't be a coincidence that people in two totally separate areas of my life were hammering me for being "combative and contrarian." As far as I could tell, there was no common denominator in these very different relationships. It seemed to behoove me to put myself in the shop for repairs.

So I signed up for therapy. At the top of my list of problems was how to make all these fights stop. "I hate fighting," I said to my shrink. "My mother insists that I intentionally provoke her. The boyfriend says I pick fights with him. Obviously, I'm not totally innocent. If I'm causing all these problems, I need to know how to knock it off."

"It is not that their opinion of you is the same. It is that *they* are the same," said the shrink, turning all my assumptions upside down, while at the same time demonstrating why she was able to charge so much money. "Your parents and your boyfriend are narcissistic, so they cannot tolerate that you are separate."

I had no idea what that meant.

My parents were a middle-class man and woman who dressed in complementary-colored permanent-press clothing. They were bound to each other by their twin passions of criticizing their offspring and picking fights with waiters. In what way could they be considered similar to my weird, off-beat, creative boyfriend in the cowboy shirt and motorcycle boots?

The shrink gave me a pile of books on narcissism to read, and when I was finished I became obsessed with buying more. Any story anyone told me about someone who was causing them problems got pushed through this new prism. "He sounds like a narcissist," I would say to everyone about everything. I began to feel like I had just joined the plot of *Invasion of the Body Snatchers* in the middle of Act 2.

Coming to a real understanding of how a narcissistic personality works took persistence. For a while, it just didn't add up. It was counterintuitive. One reason may be that some experts believe that the narcissist's emotional system becomes fatally damaged at about the age of three, maybe from something as common and inevitable as failed initial attempts at independence from Mommy. The freshly wounded three-year-old, unable to make the right adjustment, continues to cling to the infantile idea that baby and Mommy are the same all-powerful person. Sometimes he keeps clinging to this fallacy and applying it to everyone he meets for the rest of his life. So say goodbye to the development of empathy. Since everyone else is, in his view, already part of him and his system, there is no need to worry about other people's feelings. For the eternally infantile narcissist, there is only one person and one correct opinion: his.

Finally I could see how my mother (like every narcissist in good standing) was chained to a seesaw of two behavioral extremes: grandiosity and rage. Anything that happened to her inspired one reaction or the other. Things were either all good or all bad. If it wasn't summer, it was winter.

Here, at last, was an explanation for that mysterious fight on Christmas.

When my mother was allowed to be the one to pick out my clothing, it fed her grandiosity and she was pleased. But when I suggested that I had an idea I liked better than hers, I was calling her worthless and therefore humiliating her. If I wasn't feeding her grandiosity, then I was provoking her rage.

But how could I have possibly known, without talking to a shrink, that according to the unbendable rules of the narcissistic personality disorder, if I was not paying homage to my mother's taste by embracing the clothing she picked out, then in her view of things I was picking a fight? I didn't understand that narcissists never roll with the punches because I didn't know that narcissists can never be wrong. Or that, for my mother, the act of buying me a present was not about finding something I might like but a way for her to pump up her own sense of self-worth.

Had I just shut up and let her waste her money on another gathered skirt decorated with appliqué ducks that I would never wear, I would have provided her with more evidence that she had all the right answers. Instead, by thinking that my opinion mattered too, and that I was showing respect by helping her buy me something I would find useful, I had ground her face in the dirt and triggered her rage.

"In the Greek myth, Narcissus fell in love with his own reflection. But narcissism isn't actually about self-love," my shrink explained. "More like self-obsession. Anyone who isn't part of the pillar of support is part of the abyss around it."

Or, as one of my friends once explained this credo: "I'm the piece of shit the world revolves around."

Here's how it works: When a narcissist admits you into their inner circle, you haven't just made a friend, you have been annexed by an imperialist country with only one resident. Your borders have been erased. The subtext of all future interactions with this person, forevermore, will be: "What's mine is mine and what's yours is mine." Welcome to a world where there is no you!

A narcissist cannot tolerate seeing you as separate because he is a jumbo-sized three-year-old child who must be at the center of your world as well as his own. Either your needs are perfectly aligned with his or you can expect some kind of a tantrum.

Once you are involved with your narcissist, there are only two acceptable ways for you to behave with them: you become part of the admiring support team or you become the fall guy. If you are not mirroring your narcissist by reinforcing what they stand for, then you are proving that you are a separate person with a separate agenda. That means you are a threat.

So here are your choices: the Fan Club President with rose-colored glasses or the Incompetent Boob who is ruining everything and is, therefore, the enemy. If you choose the latter, you offer the narcissist a chance to release decades of pent-up unexamined rage. This works out well for them, since they are continually looking for a way to vent.

It will not, on the other hand, be so great for you.

To survive your beloved narcissist flipping out and screaming at you, it may help you to know that their personality is a mask of fake superiority covering up a deep sense of shame. All that arrogance is a fit thrown by a plus-sized infant who is furious at Mommy for not banishing every problem before it began to bother baby. It was eye-opening to realize that what I thought was a roller coaster of unpredictable behavior was instead a predictable system.

For years I could never tell if the time I spent at home was going to be unexpectedly pleasant or deteriorate into a fight that seemed to come out of nowhere. Now I learned that those unexpected fights, which looked to me like unfortunate breaks in the normal pattern of stability, *were* the pattern. The placid periods and good times were *the exception*.

Even if you have made yourself the designated Fan Club

President in the ongoing scenario with your narcissist, you can still count on their disposition to keep flip-flopping between grandiosity and rage. That's just the way it works. It has almost nothing to do with you or your choice of actions. It is based on tiny fluctuations in their mood, as they react to whatever is available, real or imagined. At two o'clock: happy and grandiose; three-fifteen: furious and raging. Within the narrow boundaries of this extremely fragile self-system (which, don't forget, was created by a frightened three-year-old), everything that is not pumping the narcissist up is trying to destroy them.

At last I had a reasonable explanation for why my brother and I, even armed with perky outfits, tidy haircuts, and carefully selected topics of conversation, always seemed to be wearing and doing and saying the wrong thing at family gatherings.

Now I had insight into what was behind three decades of embarrassing restaurant incidents in which my parents, behaving like aristocracy, treated the stammering waitstaff with barely disguised contempt.

"That's a very meager amount!" my mother would say, offended by the size of the complimentary crudités tray the waitress placed on our table. It always seemed strange to me that she would make this kind of hostile announcement rather than simply ask for a few more when she was finished. In retrospect, it is a wonder that the members of my family survived so many dinners that must have been drenched in the spit of humiliated, revenge-seeking waitpersons. Perhaps our bodies learned to embrace and process other people's saliva as an essential nutrient, like riboflavin.

Ultimately, the biggest lesson that came from my

narcissism-related reading was learning how to identify members of this annoying tribe when they are encountered in their natural habitat. Like a perfectly camouflaged salamander, almost invisible when he rests on a matching granite boulder, narcissists can be difficult to see. Especially at first, when they wrap themselves inside the charm they use to make themselves attractive in the world. This, of course, means that the charm-intensive arenas of show business and politics are as natural a habitat for narcissists as marshlands are for ducks.

Perhaps the most obvious and familiar red flag is the doting coterie of yes-men. In narcissism talk, these people are called "narcissistic supply."

Spotting a narcissist is kind of like spotting a bear. Much the way naturalists tell you not to look a grizzly bear in the eye lest it detect a challenge and attack, you are better off not staring down a narcissist. To engage them is to play by their rules. Don't forget: they are always right. Which means that the only defense against them is to remain aloof or not get involved in the first place.

Rising above my mother's baiting was an exercise in Zen I could only intermittently remember to perform. When she was in the mood to vent, I would watch her fishing around for things about me that pissed her off. Talking too fast? Check. Unflattering hairstyle? Yep. Never heard of the book she was reading? Check check check.

In the end, it was wonderful to have a clinical explanation for all of this puzzling stuff. It was also distressing to learn that there was no way for me to single-handedly control or repair all of our conflicts. Gone was the dream that handling my mother with kid gloves or talking to her honestly might transform her into someone more enlightened. Instead, the further I got into my stack of books, the clearer it was that I had to face a depressing reality: interacting with her unguardedly meant entering a one-sided conversation that would sooner or later spiral into a petty personal attack. The fantasy that she would one day accept me on my own terms was officially dead.

Since no true board-certified narcissist is ever going to change, the only variable under my control was my ability to stop reacting to her. Even then, she might initiate some fisticuffs just to stay in good form. As every book on the subject of narcissism eventually explains (in CAPS, *italics,* and **underlined with bold exclamation marks!!!**), the only method for coping is to maintain emotional distance. Change *your* expectations. There's no pleasing unpleasable people.

But forewarned is forearmed. So from that point on, when my mother provoked me, I refused to bite. When she raised one eyebrow at me and said for the millionth time, "You really don't get out to many cultural events, do you? Not the opera, not the ballet, not the theater," instead of coming back at her with "Well, neither do you. Plus, you didn't just finish writing a book," I smiled and said, "Well, no. I guess I don't." When she tried to follow it up with a list of other things I wasn't doing, I said, "Yep. Well, I guess I better go take a shower or I'm not going to get much done today, either."

And then I left the room.

It confused her when I wouldn't argue back. She could sense that I had grown more distant, that the familiar push and pull that stood in for intimacy in the dance between us had been modified without her approval. But it would have done no good to explain my motivation. Nothing I could do or say would ever make things better.

By the end of her life, I was mainly tap-dancing around her, trying not to be pulled into another pointless fight. For her, it must have been a little like being a boxer sitting in the ring, wondering why the opponent hadn't shown up.

I am grateful to my mother for inspiring me to learn about narcissism. Thanks to her, I am better equipped to function in my hometown of Los Angeles, a city so overrun with narcissists that being able to identify one is as crucial to your well-being as owning a car or a cellphone. I've developed sonarlike early-warning detection abilities, fine-tuned by decades spent as the distributor of overblown praise and the recipient of browbeatings.

I still think back proudly to a flirtation at a party a few years ago with someone who set off all my narcissism alarms. There he stood, alone, brooding, self-absorbed, and artistic, but also hilarious in a sly way. I knew instinctively, and from years of practice, that the way to draw him out of his shell was by asking probing but flattering questions, then listening to his answers with rapt attention bordering on awe. If I followed that up with extreme empathy and selfless offers of support, he would be mine. I could make love to him (or at least perform oral sex) and, if I was lucky, afterward also help clean his house and put his schedule in order.

Despite the fact that every micron of my body begged to do these things, I watched myself with amazement as the voice coming out of my face said instead, "Well, you seem like a smart guy. I'm sure you'll figure it all out."

And then I turned and went off to talk to someone else.

In my head, I received a big round of applause.

One last pearl of wisdom: If, after reading this, you are haunted by the fear that it might be you I am talking about, you are definitely *not* a narcissist. Narcissists never identify with anything that could diminish their opinion of themselves. On the other hand, if you don't recognize anything of yourself in any of the things I have mentioned, you might want to consider a career in show business or politics.

Saturday Night with Hieronymus Bosch

ATTENDING SATURDAY NIGHT'S MUCH-ADVERTISED "FETISH Ball" at the Hollywood Athletic Club seemed like the perfect idea for a story. *The laughs will come fast and furious when fish out of water meets Fetish Ball,* I said to myself. And I was right. Quickasthis I sold the idea to our big alternative weekly.

That made me happy, but I was even happier after a chef I knew told me that he attended the Fetish Ball every year and was really looking forward to it. That helped to humanize the event for me—to remind me that beneath the Félicien Rops imagery would beat the hearts of actual people, with internal organs and nervous systems and everything. I felt happier still after a large group of my friends called to say that they would love to tag along. I pictured all of us in funny outfits, talking to unusual people. And, failing that, good-natured, fun-seeking, boring people who dressed up weird. Not only would a good time be had by all, but now I was no longer worried about being pulled into a dark alley at stiletto point by Jack the Foot Worshipper.

My positive outlook continued undiminished for the rest of the week . . . right up until the Friday afternoon before the ball, when every last one of my so-called friends called to chicken out.

Apparently I would be going alone.

Okay, I said to myself, *let's take this one step at a time. No reason to panic. It's just another job covering a party in Hollywood, for crying out loud.* But still, by any measure, it seemed untoward: a woman attending a fetish ball by herself? What in God's name was I supposed to wear?

It was one thing to construct an odd, fetishy Halloweeny kind of outfit to show off at a party full of silly, ironic friends. It was quite another to get dressed up all bizarre and sexy, leave the house unescorted, drive through Hollywood in daylight, and then exit my parked car alone, still wearing the exotic getup. Further complicating things was the fact that my goal for the evening was neither to find dates nor to acquire any new deviant people in the friendship category. I did *not* want a buckle-and-zipper-laden guy in a big rubber dick suit wearing a ball gag to follow me out to my car when I left.

No, my plan, or what I laughingly thought of as one, was to be a fly on a cleanish expanse of wall so I could write some kind of hilarious essay while maintaining a safe distance. I even thought briefly about renting an actual fly costume but became concerned that there might be a fetish involving walls and flies.

So I went back to examine the original invitation. Of the choices it offered in the dress-code category—Leather, Vinyl,

Fetish Glam, Uniform, Formal, Gothic, Drag, Storybook/ Fairy Tale—Storybook/Fairy Tale seemed to offer the most possibilities. What would it mean to the room at large if I went as a character from *A Charlie Brown Christmas*? I wondered. Wasn't that a storybook by some definition? How would a nice Metro bus driver's uniform strike the other attendees? Would it give the appearance of a uniform fetish while also sending a subtle message that dangerous strangers should stay away? Or would I be busy all night long telling fetishists that no, I didn't have change for a dollar?

Of course, it was all a moot point because there were no Charlie Brown, Metro bus driver, or even Amtrak uniforms at the one costume store that was still open on the sweltering Friday afternoon before the big event. Since I had let things slide until the last possible minute, I had backed myself into the corner of this empty store and now had to face down its underwhelming inventory. Nestled among the generic beards, mustaches, false eyelashes, and superhero outfits, I now had my choice of Power Rangers, Disney princesses, and costumes related to *Shrek*. The single-digit age recommendations on the boxes for these things meant that none was going to be a very good fit for me.

Of course, there were also the "adult" costumes, which ran more along the lines of "Haight-Ashbury Honey"— a "far-out, fringe-trimmed crop top with bodacious bubble design, matching bell bottoms, and a hip and happenin' headband." A half dozen thin, reflective fuchsia-colored pieces of plastic would transform me into "one fun, foxy mamma who will have all the disco dudes ready to move," which, I supposed, was Fetish Glam, as long as my fetish was "Sad Cheap Retro Halloween Costumes That Never Sold." Or I could buy one of those mini nurse/go-go dancer uniforms just like the ones the Red Cross nurses all wore that time a hurricane hit a brothel and everyone had to take refuge in an S&M dungeon.

Waist-deep in a murky stew of anxiety and modesty, I realized that my only truly viable choice seemed to be a black velveteen Vampira gown with an attached hood. Its dark color might afford me some camouflage, allowing me to vanish into the ballroom décor like a fuzzy black sconce. On the other hand, it could have the opposite effect, since no self-respecting vampires of the twenty-first century ever seem to be caught undead in this type of getup anymore. Even with their lower body temperatures and superhuman powers, the vampires of *Twilight* and *True Blood* would hardly deign to spend an eighty-five-degree evening in a bell-sleeved, floor-length, black-hooded, polyester-blend gown in Los Angeles in July.

By now, the store was closing. I really didn't feel like doing any more shopping. So I bought the damn thing and brought it home.

The next night, I put it on, resigned to grinning and bearing it. And I did . . . for about five minutes. That was how long it took for me to feel the rivers of sweat coursing down the length of my body, from armpits to ankles. Even though looking hot always ranks at the top of costume ball criteria, this was definitely not the hot that anyone hopes to achieve.

Which left only one other category option: leather.

I owned a gray leather skirt, a black leather jacket, and brown leather boots. None of them matched. And the combination looked more preppy than dominatrix. But, fingers crossed, once I passed through the leather detectors, I would

at least be able to take the jacket off without being in viola-
tion of any fetish laws.

So I leathered up and then off I went . . . tra la la lala. Just
a girl in eighty-five-degree weather dressed in enough leather
to keep her warm in a Minnesota winter, headed for something called the Fetish Ball *all by my FUCKING SELF.*

The panic didn't set in for real until I joined the line of cars
stretching halfway down the block, slowly inching forward to
enter the parking lot. After the car ahead of me stopped to
drop off six bare-butted men, I wanted to scream to the valet
who opened my door, "How much would you charge to
come inside with me and pretend to be my date? Whatever it
is, I'll pay it! Seriously, dude. Name your price!"

Instead I composed myself, and moments later, flanked
by a guy in chaps and another in a polyvinyl cop uniform, I
strode boldly through the Hollywood Athletic Club front
doors, wearing fifteen pounds of leather and at least fifty
pounds of perspiration.

Well, to be more accurate, I strode boldly to a security
desk by the door, where I waited as my full bottle of Evian
was thrown into the garbage by two unfriendly men who
glared at me icily. They then proceeded to search every inch
of my purse with an intensity about twice that of airport security. For what? I wondered. Was a hostile security station
itself a form of a fetish? Maybe one that featured angry, impatient authority figures who made their own rules and then
had their way with you?

Once I'd been cleared, I entered a storm of strobe lights

synced up to recorded music that was roaring out of amps the size of refrigerators. The entire building seemed to vibrate like a tuning fork. I could feel it in my spinal cord. It was like sitting underneath an unusually rhythmic subway train, something to which I have never aspired. When my eyes finally got acclimated to the darkness, I discovered two things. The first was: *Shit! I got here too early. Leave it to me to once again be the only person in L.A. who takes the start time of anything seriously. Clearly no good fetishist worth their polyvinyl waist cincher would dream of showing up at a place like this before ten o'clock.* The second was that there were many different theme rooms to visit. Most were still empty, though each was so loud that I could feel the strands of my DNA unwinding.

Massively ill at ease, and needing something to do right away, I headed for the closest room with a bar to accomplish the first order of business: separating myself from my wobbly ego via inebriation.

A naughty-lady-in-a-garter-belt-and-bare-chested-man-in-tight-leather-pants-cracking-a-whip performance was taking place on a small stage about ten feet from where I ordered a glass of white wine. That I was the entire audience for this bit of S&M cabaret was unnerving, to say the least. It was much too early and I was far too sober to face the responsibility of having to fake orgasm on behalf of some much larger crowd of people who hadn't arrived yet. So I took advantage of the opportunity to grab a few cocktail napkins to wad up into balls and stuff into my ears. Then I wandered back out into the still mostly empty entry hall to watch the happy fetishists trickle in the front door.

Positioning myself against a back wall, clinging to a yellow legal pad like it was a life raft while pretending to sip from my now empty glass, I heard an odd kind of parade commentary running in my mind.

Oh look. The orthodontia contingent has arrived, in their polished and gleaming bite-plate headgear. And right behind them . . . why, it's the Butterfly People! Followed by the solemn precision marching of the Irritable Leash Brigade. Let's give them all a nice hand! No wonder they look angry. It takes a lot of hard work and practice for primates to maintain that crawling position. And here come . . . the Ancient Greeks, for centuries a Fetish Ball favorite, the timeless formality of their togas complementing as well as contrasting with their startling lack of undergarments. My, but it's a nice turnout this year for those swashbuckling crowd-pleasers, the Pirate Brigade! Carefully tended facial hair, dangerous accessories . . . is there anything these guys don't have? Wow! Will you look at who has just walked in the door! Everyone's favorite: DIAPER BOY! Behold how his pale, naked torso shimmers in the black light as he waddles through the security checkpoint. . . . Hey. How come they stopped me but they didn't stop him?

Heading for the main ballroom, I became preoccupied with the plushie standing near the entrance. Dressed in a sad-eyed panda suit embellished with angel wings, he stood unmoving as scantily clad women came up to pet him. *Poor little sad-eyed, harmless, adorable panda angel . . . all he ever wanted was to cuddle! Come sit on his lap and give the big panda a hug! Just remember to pretend you don't feel the sweaty erection of the guy inside the suit as he pushes against you, same way you pretended you didn't when you slow-danced with that pale creepy boy with the clammy hands at your junior high dinner dance.*

By eleven o'clock the main ballroom, a dark, cavernous chamber with a big stage on which a continuous live burlesque show seemed to be cycling in an endlessly repeating loop, was nearly full. None of the many provocatively costumed attendees in their restrictive, revealing outfits or super-high platform stilettos seemed at all challenged by the gale-force velocity of the amplified sound waves. Clustered together and towering above me on the ballroom floor, they formed one of the few crowds of people collectively over seven feet tall who showed no signs at all of playing basketball.

Apparently the idea of conversation was not a fetish that interested anyone, as it was almost impossible to hear even a shouting human voice in the midst of the vibrating roar. "What are you supposed to be?" I tried yelling at a white-haired man in his sixties dressed in a mysterious robe-and-jockstrap ensemble topped by an asymmetrical crown.

"What?"

"WHAT ARE YOU SUPPOSED TO BE?"

"KING NEPTUNE! I HAVE A FISH FETISH!" he screamed back, dangling a fishing line with a Caucasian-colored latex dildo hooked onto it in front of my face. Unable to think of a witty retort of any kind, I smiled, nodded, and moved on, wondering whether his outfit had started with the dildo or the crown.

Talking was also out of the question for the vaguely human creature who lay on the floor breathing through a plastic strawlike tube, trapped between layers of form-fitted black latex sheeting stretched across a rectangular frame. He or she looked like an oversized, poorly labeled liverwurst packaged for travel to a distant planet. I had stumbled into the latex room. Against one wall was a platform stage on which latex-clad women, like shiny intergalactic girlfriends of the Fantastic Four, were cavorting and striking threatening poses. Nevertheless the full-enclosure vacuum bed on which liverwurst person was stretched and shrink-wrapped into complete immobility seemed to be a bigger draw than the sexy ladies. A crowd of people stood around, staring quietly at this unidentifiably gendered person trapped like a gnat in a spiderweb. For a childhood asthma sufferer like myself, something about seeing the restricted oxygen supply being meted out by the tube was so unnerving that I stumbled backward into a light switch and accidentally turned on all the lights in the room. "Lights on" was definitely a fetish no one here seemed to like in the least.

Beating a hasty retreat back to the crowded hallway, I tripped forward into a tall, thin man in a fifteenth-century brocaded French cavalry uniform with knee-high boots, brandishing a riding crop. He smiled. It was my friend the chef, having the time of his life. "What are you so freaked about?" he shouted, reading the anxiety on my face. "Ninety-nine percent of the people here are not in the least bit dangerous. You want to know who *is* dangerous here? See those four jocks in T-shirts and jeans over there who probably snuck in?"

"How do you know they snuck in?" I asked him.

"Well, they could never have gotten past security in those clothes," he replied. "*They* are the kind of guys who scare me. The straight ones. They might get drunk and hurt somebody."

By now, both floors of the place were filled with wall-to-wall revelers. Each room had been transformed into a seething holding pen for the extras from a James Ensor painting. As the hour grew later, the crowds kept getting bigger and bigger, until the whole place was a simmering, pulsating petri dish of human eccentricity...as if Hieronymus Bosch had thrown a party in which only the species with the most aberrant mating habits were permitted to attend: only the frigate birds, the bat-eating centipedes, the night-swimming scorpions, the cannibalistic, sexually doomed praying mantises. And as befits nature at its strangest, every interaction came complete with an elaborately staged and carefully choreographed tango. Leave it to humans to take something as basic as courtship rites and add details so complicated that they required the invention, manufacture, and international distribution of polyvinyl chloride.

I had begun the evening with every intention of maintaining a spirit of amused journalistic tolerance. I considered myself a graduate of Basic Freak Culture 101, having studied in both Los Angeles and New York. I took it for granted that I had long since lost the ability to be truly rattled by the entertainment ideas of my fellow humans. Therefore, I expected to find tonight's event surprisingly engaging, titillating, and funny. That's how it usually works with me: I approach skeptically, then empathy takes over, and next thing I know, I'm pricing latex underwear online.

What I'd never expected was for so many of these costumes to look like a road map to someone's childhood abuse. Where I'd predicted benign eccentricity, I began instead to hear unanswered questions: Was that pierced guy in the harness with the spike-studded neck stretcher the victim of a violent father? That poker-faced, obese, freckled girl in the tutu who sat obediently chained to the feet of the biker in the leather chaps, her pale legs folded under her like bolster pillows—what frightening, long-buried scenario from her childhood was playing and replaying in her head as she knelt there? Was this a fantasy that came from a lifetime of social rejection? Or was acting sad part of the way she showed a sadistic biker beau that she cared about him and was having fun? What sequence of disturbing events had led a guy who usually got up in the morning and worked at the window of a bank to come to this stifling-hot room dressed like a ten-year-old girl in an Alice in Wonderland pinafore, knee-high white stockings, and Mary Janes? Did he have a disturbed mother, like the woman that raised Sybil, who'd forced him to dress like a little girl? These kinds of questions began to sand the funny edge right off of things for me.

In the name of thoroughness, I had promised myself that I'd stay long enough to see at least one of everything. But by midnight, I felt an urge to slow down a little. I decided to take a break in the quietest room I could find, which turned out to be a second-floor library, empty but for a row of folding chairs against one wall. What a blessing, I thought as I took a seat, to see that nothing at all was going on here. Now I could indulge my own favorite fetish: retreating to an empty room during a party, just before sneaking out the back door. Or that was my plan until I was joined by a woman with a parasol and ruffled bloomers, looking like she'd stepped out of *Sunday in the Park with George*. She followed behind a Ted Bundy doppelgänger who was leading her by a leash attached to a dog collar. The two of them set up shop on the unused chairs about ten feet from where I was sitting, then began to go through the paces of an S&M (unless it was B&D) playlet, for which I appeared to be the designated audience. At least that was a conclusion I couldn't help but reach, since I was the only other person in the room.

This raised an etiquette dilemma that Emily Post had never touched on: When you're the only one in the audience for a spanking demonstration that involves a bare-butted woman who is looking directly into your eyes, how long must you sit quietly, pretending to be enthralled, before you're permitted to sneak out? I was reminded of the time an actress I knew insisted that I attend her one-woman show. I put off going for as long as I could. Then finally, during the last week of the run, I gave in out of politeness, intending to sit in the last row of the theater until things became unbearable. That was before I realized that no one else had bought a ticket that day. I was the only audience member, therefore I had no choice but to commit to enjoying the show till its very end. Yet, looking back, my friend and her tale of spiritual awakening was entertainment of the highest form compared to this Bo Peep–meets–Ted Bundy chair-based one-act psychodrama. Many are the times I have thought, while watching a porno movie, that I was glad I didn't know anything about the cast. This turned out to be a detailed refresher course in that feeling.

So there I sat, trying to maintain an amused but not too enthusiastic expression as I watched Ted Bundy teach Bo Peep an allegorical lesson. I tried to look reasonably appreciative to spare them the embarrassment of bombing (or was that what they wanted? Who really knew with this crowd?) yet not so interested that Mr. Bundy would urge me to join the festivities. Then, after about eight minutes, I decided to risk hoping that they might interpret my departure as that of a canny sadist denying them the pleasure of being watched and not a bad review. I got up and walked rapidly toward the door.

This time I was wildly relieved to rejoin the pulsating *carnavale*-like throb of the million-odd tribe members out in the hall, as I made my way back toward the stairs, past young nude men dressed only in chaps, past the old geezers in G-strings (where oh where do they get all that confidence?), past a bare-chested guy with a disco ball on his head, arm in arm with his partner, a guy dressed only in a truss. I pushed onward, onward toward the main exit, past the woman in the Little Miss Muffet outfit who looked like Judy Tenuta but wasn't. Past the woman in the rubber dress who looked like Margaret Cho and was. ("Hi, Margaret!" "Whaat?" "I said, 'HI, MARGARET!'" "Hi, Merrill! What did you say? I can't hear you!") Onward past dozens and dozens of women in shiny PVC separates with their grommeted, spiky-rubber-and-leather-clad pals, all of them out for an evening of hotness, extreme foot pain, and photo-opportunity kissing.

Look—there's a man with a whip and a bridle and a full-body harness that is meant as some kind of a pony getup! And right next to him is a woman with a broom and a dustpan! Some sort of anal-retentive, obsessive-compulsive thing? Finally a weird fetish that I do understand. Oh wait . . . she's actually cleaning up.

And so, at one o'clock in the morning, I said goodbye to the Fetish Ball, knowing it was not even close to being over, relieved to feel the fresh air outside the building and so happy to get back into my car that I almost cried. My body continued vibrating and buzzing like an electric razor as I decompressed on the drive back home, even as I marveled at the sheer madness, absurdity, and creativity of my species, the only creatures on the planet that do anything remotely this preposterous. We, the humans, who contemplate dark matter for our work and then, for our relaxation, want to be immobilized by latex, tickled with a cat-o'-nine-tails, and fed our air through a tiny tube. No imaginary life on any theoretical other planet could be any odder or more full of strange details than this. Maybe each and every male bowerbird attracts a mate by decorating his nest with an individually chosen assortment of beautiful berries, flowers, shiny pebbles, and insect wings, like an ornithological equivalent of a Las Vegas hotelier; but name another creature who volunteers to wear a bridle, a harness, and a horse tail and who also *isn't in any way, shape, or form a horse!*

As I merged onto the freeway and left Hollywood in my exhaust, I felt like I always do at the end of a vacation: happy to have gained more perspective, but stressed. And glad that I lived somewhere else.

When I Was Jack Kerouac

By eighth grade, at North Miami Junior High, I was under the impression that I was a made man. I had just been inducted into a secret sorority run by my many best friends: a group of clothing-label-obsessed girls who all lived in beautiful homes that were right on the water. We were thirteen and only too aware that spending seven hours a day together at school and then talking to each other on the phone for a few more hours at night offered barely enough time to discuss and analyze how many pairs of Pappagallo shoes each of us had.

Pappagallo shoes were, for us, many things: a wardrobe anchoring point, a yardstick of fashion savvy, a sought-after collectible, a weekend shopping destination. In our group, my personal supply fell embarrassingly short. I had only two pairs, both patent leather slip-ons. I was unable to raise my total because my mother didn't like the idea of a bunch of eighth-grade girls telling her what kind of shoes she ought to be buying for her kid. She preferred to shop at Pixx Shoes for Less, where we could buy five knockoff pairs of Pappagallos for the price of one real pair. "They're the same damn shoes," she would argue. "All the stores buy them from the same warehouse and then they sew in their own label. There is absolutely no difference."

She couldn't have been more wrong.

My friends prided themselves on being able to spot a whole range of nearly invisible details that separated a knockoff from an original. If a single stitch was the wrong shape or color or in the wrong place, they would catch it. To be seen in fake Pappagallos was a bigger shame than owning none at all.

"Maddie has twenty-three pairs," my friends would announce every time her name came up in conversation. And the rule held for all of us: "Deedee has sixteen. Kathy has eleven." They had memorized the stats for everyone's closet the way the boys memorized home runs and RBIs. And in this way, they provided me with a measure of safety. As long as I followed their rules and regulations to the letter, I would always fit in.

I was proud of the way my sorority sisters were fashion geniuses. At our most memorable sorority meeting, someone's aunt—a part-time model—came to offer us her helpful hints for living a better life. The evening began with her strolling slowly down the aisles between the desks in a borrowed classroom, addressing each of us individually to let us know, for our own good, if we were "too fat" or "too thin." Not that any evening ever needed more, but this one ended with an exhaustive lesson in eyebrow shaping. "You want to take a pencil and outline the arch, then pluck *around* it," she advised, while I sighed with relief at having managed to avoid being labeled as too fat. Luckily for me, I had grown nine inches that year.

I had only begun to scratch the surface of this wellspring of social expertise and grooming advice when in the middle of ninth grade, my mother and father called my brother and me into the living room one evening after dinner to explain that the family was moving to California. In that awful moment, the bottom fell out of not just my brand-new plucking studies but my hard-won secret-society standing as well.

California threw me for a loop. First of all, there were no Pappagallo shoes, period. It was hard to imagine, but no. There were none for sale anywhere. I conducted an exhaustive telephone search.

Even more disturbing, the cute girls at my new high school were working from a whole different style catalogue connected to surfing, a complete mystery to me even though I had been living exactly as close to an ocean in Florida as I now was in California. But back in North Miami, when we talked about "the beach," we were referring to the best shopping mall for buying Pappagallos.

A radical reassessment of everything I knew to be true was now in order.

"I am the world's most thoroughly out-of-it teenager," I fretted in my diary shortly after we moved to the other coast. "At North Miami Junior High, all I wanted was to be a member of the popular group. But since I got to California, I am no longer interested. I guess I'm the big weirdo here.

Plus I am shy and self-conscious around boys, which is mainly their fault because they don't like me and I know it."

I wasn't really telling the whole truth. Where boys were concerned, at North Miami Junior High I had been having the same exact problem. I wasn't sure why this was, but it definitely wasn't because I didn't care. I was always deeply in love with someone. Unfortunately these relationships were never reciprocal. And the situation was made even more difficult by the fact that the boys I loved most I had never actually met.

"If you looked at last year's reports I was positively swooning over RG," I had written back in North Miami in the beginning of ninth grade about a guy I had never talked to. "I got goose bumps just looking at him. But it is interesting to note that he means nothing to me now. Even less, perhaps. Now I like Michael. I wish he'd like me. But of course he really hasn't even met me yet."

Next thing I knew, there I was, trapped in California: three thousand miles away and, socially speaking, back at square one. Not only did none of the boys at my brand-new school know of my existence, but there was no secret sorority of fashion wizards who had my back. For the first few months, I drifted, briefly hanging out with the Mormon girl down the street and her friends from church, who called each other "Brother" and "Sister." But while floundering in a world where I clearly did not belong, I began to detect a more interesting social strata inside the drama class I had taken as an elective. Not only did it include appealing members of both sexes but it also came with its own intriguing dress code.

It took me a couple of weeks of scrutinizing these kids to get the lay of the land. Then I made a run at emulating two beautiful, haunted-looking drama class seniors, who wore black turtlenecks, black tights, dangling earrings, dark eyeliner, and long, straight hair parted down the middle. They were the pale, hollow-cheeked, teenage avant-garde devotees of every artistic rebellious subculture the United States had to offer at that point: part Greenwich Village, part Haight-Ashbury, part Carnaby Street. "Nonconformists" was what my mother called them, with a sneer. I wasn't sure what that meant, but I wanted to be just like them.

So I dove headlong into an overnight transformation from sorority girl to jaded boho chick, hoping to make it instantly appear that I'd been like this for years. When one of my new role models helped ease my transition by giving me a couple of pairs of her old dangly earrings, I was so appreciative that I tried to sit at my desk exactly the same way she sat at hers, bouncing one shoe off the end of my foot. If I could have gotten her mother, who was an author, to agree to let me join their bloodline in progress, I would have turned my back on my own family in a heartbeat. Especially since I was already very concerned that the stable, boring lives of my middle-class parents were fatally undermining my artistic credibility.

"I come from a happy, middle-class family of above-average intelligence and we live in the most supremely mundane and mediocre of all possible horrible suburbias," I wrote in my diary in the winter of my sophomore year. "I don't know why I used the word 'happy' because it is an environment that has never made me happy. I don't think, feel, or want what the rest of my family wants. I don't even want to want what they want. I hate going on long drives with them and listening to my father explain about how boys are attracted to feminine, neatly dressed young ladies who take pride in their appearances."

I was banking on my father being wrong, because that definitely wasn't my agenda anymore, even though that pesky boy problem was far from under control. "The first and only relationship I have ever had with a boy was this year," I wrote, "if you can even call it a relationship."

I was talking about Bob, a long-haired, redheaded, freckle-faced, pre-drowning Brian Jones look-alike who went to another school. On the bright side, Bob represented progress, since I had, in fact, actually met him! He was friends with my new drama-crowd friend Ned, a guy so cool that he had an American flag for a bedspread. (And don't forget: this was the sixties, when a kid using an American flag for room décor meant rebellion and nihilism, not conservative family values.) Ned was a dazzling compendium of hip, artistic details. He wrote with a Rapidograph pen, using colored ink. Pretty soon, so did I. He wore a real navy peacoat with jeans and a scarf and a cap and motorcycle boots. I got as many of those as my mother would pay for. And because he worked after school in the scenery department of a small community theater, I volunteered my services there, too.

And there was Bob: a shy, morose, peace-pin-wearing conscientious objector. Once I learned he could draw, I didn't need to know more. I was deeply in love.

But it was after he held my hand during a Smothers Brothers–Pete Seeger concert at Stanford that our love was firmly etched onto the pages of history. Eventually that turned into a kiss that played in a constantly repeating loop in my head, uninterrupted, day and night. No need for any more thoughts. Just this one was a full-time job.

"Last night I felt like, 'God, he is so neat. I just love him,' " I wrote in my diary the next day. "Although I doubt I really meant love. But it sure seemed like it at the time. Okay, yeah, I meant it."

Still, despite my unquenchable passion, nothing in my flimsy fifteen-year-old playbook gave me the slightest clue about how to transform him from a one-time make-out into my boyfriend forever.

I was briefly encouraged when he turned up unannounced one night to visit me at my parents' house. As I showed him my record collection—which was, oddly enough, identical to Ned's—I knew exactly what I wanted to see happen: a riveting conversation on topics of deep personal importance, perhaps involving the roots of the blues, that would somehow lead to a lot more passionate kissing. Unfortunately, a few minutes after I started to play him my new Sonny Terry and Brownie McGhee album, Bob fell asleep facedown on my bedroom floor. At first I was puzzled. Then I was touched: *Aw! See how relaxed he is around me!* Then I was puzzled again: *Why would he come all the way over here to fall asleep?* Then I was rattled, unable to decode what a sixteen-year-old boy passed out on the floor of my bedroom might possibly mean in the bigger romantic overview. "Last night I spent one of the most depressing evenings I have ever experienced," I wrote in my diary. "Maybe I gained a little insight into things, but I doubt it. It's strange, but the more I am with

Bob, the less I seem to know him. It is impossible for me to determine ahead of time just how he will act around me. Not that I would ever want him to be predictable. It's just that . . . I never know what is going on inside his head. I would love to know what Bob considers this relationship to be. Am I his girlfriend or am I just his friend? Does he always make out with all his friends in cars? Tonight as he was lying on the floor of my room, asleep, how did he expect me to act? When he woke up and I sat with him, he seemed very far away. I want him to like me so bad but I never seem to know what he wants. Oh fuck. Now no one likes me again."

The dilemma I was facing was obvious. Unfortunately, the solution was not. What oh what did I have to do to rewrite this story with a better ending?

How could I become the kind of charismatic figure that could inspire Bob to stay awake in my presence? I didn't know where to turn.

I turned to Jack Kerouac.

A few times a week, after school, my new best friend, Debby, and I would put on our shredded cutoffs, our striped T-shirts, our leather sandals, our leather earrings and bracelets (which Debbie had made), and ride our bikes to Kepler's bookstore, about two miles from my parents' house, to hang out. I loved this bookstore. It had all the right cultural trappings: enormous weird posters of French cinema stars, an espresso machine, a dish full of peace symbols for sale next to the cash register. And, for an infinite amount of extra bonus points, it was owned by someone named Ira who was said to be a close personal friend of Joan Baez's. That was the fewest degrees of separation between me and someone awesome... ever.

I spent hours and hours browsing through the aisles of Kepler's, picking out books to read based solely on the artwork they chose for their covers. But what I was really doing was searching for something... a novel, a play, a poem that could offer me a vivid diagram of who I should be. I was looking for a three-dimensional blueprint, a manifesto on how to be a real authentic artist and therefore nothing at all like my parents. Because the name Jack Kerouac was mentioned in most of the roundups of things that were hip, when I saw his books featured on a front table, I was drawn to them.

The only title I recognized was his most famous book, *On the Road.* I almost didn't buy it because of the cover illustration: a pouty watercolor sketch of an Ann-Margret lookalike with a bare midriff and a bubble hairdo posing, all sultry, in front of a series of smaller pencil drawings of guys with slicked-back hair in short-sleeved shirts playing trumpets. Jazz trumpets sounded like mosquito music to me. Those cover graphics looked wrong, like illustrations from a spread in *TV Guide.* And the people in them didn't resemble anyone I would want to know, let alone be.

But for some reason, I took a chance and bought that book and *Dharma Bums* anyway. And once I got into them, I found a window into a way of being that had never occurred to me before: madness.

"The only people for me are the mad ones," Kerouac wrote, doing for the word "mad" what Holden Caulfield had done for "goddam." "The ones who are mad to live, mad to talk, mad to be saved, desirous of everything at the same time, the ones who never yawn or say a commonplace thing, but burn, burn, burn, like fabulous yellow roman candles exploding like spiders across the stars!"

There it was. The missing integer: a wired, crazy energy that would cause me to live every moment at a higher frequency. I had been sleepwalking through life, a follower, a sheep. But now I could see that it was madness that would set me apart. It was madness that would wake up Bob and make him take notice.

"Here's to the crazy ones," Kerouac wrote. "The misfits. The rebels. The trouble-makers ... The ones who see things differently. They're not fond of rules, and they have no respect for the status-quo ... Because they change things. They push the human race forward. And while some may see them as the crazy ones, we see genius. Because the people who are crazy enough to think they can change the world, are the ones who do."

Perfect. This was so exactly a description of the new me: one of those people who never said a commonplace thing and was crazy enough to change the world. There was no way Bob would be able to resist an amazing maniac like me whose melodic laugh was "a triumphant call to the demon god." In fact, Bob might have to get in line. Plenty of artsy souls who were younger, hipper, and a lot cuter than Jack Kerouac's old-guy author's photo would probably want to be with me, too. I would be their inspiration, their muse. Though, of course, I would be an artist, too. I would put on my leather jewelry and my thrift store wide-brimmed hat and go burn burn burning like Roman spiders across the stars.

Having arrived at a plan, I felt I needed to get it all done instantly.

"'Sal, we gotta go and never stop going till we get there,'" I underlined in my copy of *On the Road*. "'Where we going, man?' 'I don't know but we gotta go.'"

I was ready. Well, almost ready, since I couldn't apply for my driver's license for another year. It was not going to be as easy to go screaming into the night without access to a car. It was also not going to be as easy to do something else that was clearly essential for my new identity: hit the bars. But dammit, that wouldn't hold back a mad genius like me! Especially now that I knew that what I had to do to join my artistic destiny was get roaring drunk. And not half-assed, like the time I siphoned off some of my father's Cutty Sark. No, I was planning on full-out "barefooted, wild-haired, in the red fire dark, singing, swigging wine, spitting, jumping, and running—that's the way to live" drunk. I would reach "the point of ecstasy that I always wanted to reach, which was the complete step across chronological time into timeless shadows…where all the angels dove off and flew into the holy void of uncreated emptiness, the potent and inconceivable radiances shining in bright Mind Essence, innumerable lotuslands falling open in the magic mothswarm of heaven."

Okay, maybe I had no idea what any of that actually meant. But as long as I didn't have to take a test on it or listen to any jazz trumpeters in short-sleeved shirts play mosquito music during it, I could see no reason why it wouldn't all work out perfectly.

Getting mad roaring drunk was my main priority that night when Debby and I took off on our crazy mad bikes to attend an amazing maniac genius party at the empty house of someone whose parents were said to be out of town. Since I was already Sal Paradise, Debby had to be Dean Moriarty, but without the penchant for stealing cars or making love to two different real gone women in hotel rooms on different sides of town at the same time. (At least we definitely knew how to sit on the bed cross-legged facing each other, to "communicate with absolute honesty and absolute completeness everything on our minds" like Sal did with someone or other.)

Most important of all: Bob was supposed to be at this party. Beautiful mad genius holy man Bob with his Brian Jones haircut and his inconceivable radiances. Would he actually talk to me like he remembered that we had made out? Would he be awake enough to join me in some spitting, jumping, and running?

This time I wouldn't allow him to lie on the floor facedown and fall asleep. I would demand to know what he wanted out of life, the way Sal Paradise used to ask his gonest girls, while also refusing, for their own good, to let them yawn.

The party seemed to be hosted by a boy named Melvin, who didn't actually live in the house in which it was being held. He was rumored to be half Native American, sending his holy madman ratings into the stratosphere. How he came to have access to this house that belonged to someone else's parents, I didn't know and didn't care.

Not much was going on when I arrived. It didn't even look like anyone knew there was going to be a party in this standard-issue lower-middle-class living room full of unexceptional furniture. The kids I knew were all standing around in the kitchen, but there was nothing to eat or drink until everyone chipped in whatever money they had to give to

Melvin to give to a guy he knew who hung out in front of a liquor store. That guy would definitely buy us whatever kind of alcohol we wanted. How gone amazing maniac madman was that?

I wasn't present at the sacred moment of the beverage purchase, but I was definitely there when the many tall cans of Schlitz malt liquor and the largest bottle of Gordon's vodka in North America arrived.

Schlitz was what everyone else was drinking, straight from the can. But Jack Kerouac had whispered in my ear that vodka was the best way to step across chronological time into the inconceivable radiances shining in bright Mind Essence. I wasn't sure how much I needed to get to the magic moth-swarm, so I poured myself a full sixteen-ounce glass.

I drank half of it in one swallow, then shuddered as I waited for the moment when I would join the spirit of the angels diving. *Damn,* I remember thinking as I open-throated the rest of the glass in order to minimize the agony of the horrible flavor, *I'm still not drunk. I wonder what I'm doing wrong. I better drink another glass.*

That was also when I realized that I did kind of feel a bit more relaxed than I had at the start of the evening. Definitely giddier, and more ready to throw back my head and unleash my mad demon laugh. Now I knew what I had to do. I made a beeline for Bob, who was standing with a group of guys in the kitchen, sipping his can of Schlitz as he leaned against the refrigerator.

"I need to talk to you," I said, thrilled when he seemed amenable. He was definitely easier to talk to when he was vertical and experiencing consciousness.

I can't remember what slick set of moves I used next to

encourage Bob to make out with me again. I suspect that the sixteen ounces of vodka I chugged had loosened me up just a little. I briefly felt as though I'd been given a head-to-toe shot of novocaine.

Sadly, I got to live only a very few seconds of my new-found ecstasy, because no sooner did I lie down on the floor on top of my beloved than the vodka hit me like a poorly built ship crashing into a rock.

The next thing I knew someone was helping me out of the backseat of an unfamiliar car at the edge of my parents' driveway. Whoever was behind the wheel was giving me instructions. "Just say hi to your parents, go into your room, and go to sleep," a guy, perhaps Melvin, was saying over and over and over.

"Okay," I said, realizing for the first time that I was unsteady on my feet as I attempted to walk away from the car and head toward either the holy void of uncreated emptiness or the most supremely mundane and mediocre of all possible horrible suburban ranch-style houses.

When I arrived at the front door, I hesitated. I had a better idea. I could go into the garage and sleep in my mother's car until I got my bearings. That way, when I woke up, I would be refreshed and better equipped to deal with both the stability of the intrinsic Mind and the unpredictable moods of my parents.

It all seemed to be working so well, until the frantic piercing voices of my mother and father interrupted my reverie.

"What are you doing out here?" they both shouted as they got into my mother's car in the middle of the night to drive to the police department. Apparently shocked to find me asleep in the backseat, they were far too hysterical to appreciate the subtle but effective way that I was moving the human race forward.

During the death march from the car back into the house, I remembered the original orders from the mad holy man who had driven me home.

"Okay," I said to my father, who just stood there, staring and shaking his head. "Well, I'm going to my room now to go to sleep."

"Whose *clothes* are you wearing?" my mother asked, her voice drained of everything but her barely contained rage. And when I looked down, I saw not innumerable lotus-lands falling open but an unfamiliar pair of button-fly blue Levi's with a tear in one knee and a man's white T-shirt.

"Um, I don't know," I said, trying to appear blasé, as though it was a commonplace thing for me to not recognize the clothes I was wearing. "Well! Okay!" I said. "Good night!"

"Are you *drunk*?" my mother asked me.

"No, not at all," I said. "Tired. Gotta get some sleep!"

My parents stood there, glaring at me. But instead of taking me into the kitchen to interrogate me under a bare light-bulb, as I feared, they watched, unamused, as I rushed into my bedroom and closed the door.

Lying in my bed, I reminded myself that parental alien-ation was a desirable new part of my mad-to-live trouble-maker persona. Maybe if they stopped speaking to me for a long enough time, I would have a shot at being an artist after all.

Right about then was when I discovered that apparently the earth had slipped off its axis and begun spinning at a right angle.

My parents refused to talk to me for the next four days.

Luckily, during that time I was allowed to make a very confusing set of phone calls to my equally hungover friends so I could piece together what had happened after I started making out with Bob that magical night. During the holy void of uncreated emptiness, they told me, I had begun puking all over myself.

Could that be true? I had? Had I buried my one true love in a geyser of puke?

Maybe there was some way he had scooted out before the dam burst? I was too afraid to find out. Oh please, God, let that be what had happened. Let him have been lying *on top* of me at that point. Let him have sensed the danger and rolled to safety before I erupted.

Meanwhile, I tried to comfort myself with the knowledge that Sal and Dean would have found poetry in an evening of necking and puking. Talk about total madness. Maybe in my drunkenness I'd done the "monkey dance in the streets of life."

And then, as luck would have it, the school week began with an omen: the principal announced that there was a special mandatory assembly for the whole student body featuring a speaker from Alcoholics Anonymous. After some generic opening remarks, the AA representative gave each of us a checklist to fill out that would help us gauge how far down the road to alcoholism we had traveled thus far.

"Have you ever been drunk to the point of blacking out?" was one of the first questions he asked. "If you answered yes, than you are an alcoholic."

I felt a chill run through my body. Really? I was? Had I somehow gone from a friendless teetotaling transfer student, suffocating in a stifling airless suburbia, to a certified alcoholic in one day without even getting to make a barefooted, wild-haired, in the red fire dark pit stop at the burning stars? From a dullard with no love life and no creative credentials to a messed-up tragic drunken wastrel whose diseased biology would spiral her into the gutter? Just like that? They weren't kidding when they said it caught you fast.

Even worse, I had managed to screw up my second and probably last chance to make out with Bob. He had done his part this time. He'd shown up awake. He had offered me an opportunity to prove to him that I was such an inspirational life force that he could not live without me. He had come to the party ready to make out. And I had ruined everything.

No love affair, no matter how majestic or perfect, could go from a kiss to a fountain of vomit and survive. That was the awful truth. I had torn down, annihilated, crushed all that we had worked so hard to build by being a sad shipwreck... an alcoholic. Fifteen and my life was ruined. On and on and into the endless forever of night.

Bobby

LET'S TALK ABOUT YOU FOR A MINUTE.

Let's say you had a rather long romantic liaison a few decades ago, one that started back when you were in your twenties. For the sake of argument, let's call the guy you dated Bobby.

The relationship with Bobby didn't work out too well because most people in their twenties are not that smart about love. It's hard to combine clearheaded thinking and good common sense with postcollegiate identity crises and binge drinking. How were you to know then that the behaviors you regarded as "living life to the fullest" would one day appear, almost to the letter, in a list of the symptoms of mental illness?

In your case, you thought your big mistake was mixing work and love. Sure, you'd heard people say, "Don't shit where you eat," but that never made sense because the way you saw it, every good restaurant has an excellent restroom. And besides, wasn't combining two things you like to make a third thing you love the kind of good idea that brought us chocolate milk?

So let's say that when you met Bobby, he was just turning thirty-one. Bobby! Smart, funny, cute, talented, and right in the middle of a divorce from the nice girl he married when he was a hard-drinking, hard-partying frat boy. What if you laughed when you realized he was exactly the type you never would have dated in college because even back then you weren't amused by watching guys crush beer cans against their foreheads? But now, in your late twenties, you and Bobby seemed to have as many similarities as differences. What if you had so much chemistry with Bobby that the very idea that you would have shunned him when you were in college now sounded comical and small-minded?

Okay, maybe friends who'd known Bobby longer than you had warned you from the beginning that he was a risky choice because, since his marriage had ended, he had scored an impressive number of notches on the bedpost he would have had if he wasn't living in a one-room apartment and sleeping on a broken box spring. But for argument's sake, let's say you got through this unnervingly juvenile period by believing these were only the early days of a brand-new relationship. How could there not be greater stability ahead? Doesn't everything in life have to muddle through a shaky beginning? Besides, you were so excited by the way you and Bobby had begun to deepen your bond by collaborating. Obviously, Bobby could find tons of girls to date, but how many of them could help redefine and expand his business? And what if this was something you did eagerly because combining work and love seemed like a very good example of the old milk-and-chocolate-combining model to you back then? After all, sharing a studio and having art shows with your art school boyfriend had been one of the best things about your last relationship.

So then what if, over time, this collaboration got more intense as Bobby's business continued to get larger? And what if this collaboration went on to bring Bobby a lot of success? What if it was the kind of success that put Bobby at the very top of his field of endeavor, whatever that was: manufacturing frozen pizzas, selling foreign imports, managing a hedge fund, running a TV show, whatever. And what if it was not just the "pay your bills and start a savings account" type of success but more the "purchase multiple dwellings and many sports cars" variety? You'd think that this would have been a triumphant moment for you and Bobby, where you sat giddily on the top of a mountain and toasted your fabulous good fortune.

But what if Bobby had never been the type of person to celebrate good fortune, not even when he was a freewheeling fraternity boy? And therefore, what if success didn't change his relentless negativity? What if Bobby was the kind of guy who was able to somehow view your mutual achievements as failures? What if all the success only made him depressed and agitated?

Ha! But you know you! You always think you can come up with the solution to everything! So then what if, in your search for a remedy for Bobby's unhappiness, it occurred to you that maybe your idea of combining work and love was the core of the problem? Of course you would think this. You were trained by your culture and by your gender to value love over work. After all, isn't love what makes the world go round? So then what if that led you to conclude that the best thing you could do would be to step away from this business you and Bobby had built...selling discount cleaning supplies or running a French restaurant or dropping watermelons off of buildings...whatever it was you guys did together. It made sense to think that if you avoided the line of fire at work, the time you spent together at home would become a safe haven. Obviously, it wouldn't occur to you that there was one big glaring incorrect integer in this equation, kind of like the inherent flaw in the chocolate-plus-milk formula. What if you had failed to notice that time at work was the only time that mattered to Bobby?

Then what if, even after signs that this wasn't working too well, you stayed the course, trying to prove that your theory was correct and something good would eventually come of it all? What if you hung around the house, cooking exotic Craig Claiborne recipes from *The New York Times Cookbook,* until one day when you intercepted some suspicious letters written in a big, loopy, young girl's handwriting that Bobby claimed had been sent to him by "a crazy person"? Maybe you tried to believe him, even though the letters sounded more feebleminded and adolescent than they did psychotic. After all, "letters from a crazy person" wasn't an unreasonable explanation in those days, because part of the success you and Bobby had wrought in your business involved the unwanted intrusion of unstable customers whose clinically diagnosed psychiatric disorders occasionally inspired them to break into your house.

But still . . . what if right after that there were a bunch of other awful things that caused the whole house of cards you had built with Bobby to topple? Like inconsistent remarks when he called from his office at the cardboard box factory or the lumberyard or the Home Depot or the broadcast facility or the haircut emporium or wherever it was that he worked? What if it now was becoming clear that love and work had again united for Bobby, but this time you were not part of either one?

Well, that would be rather upsetting and even heartbreaking for most people. But let's say that over a period of years, once the inevitable breakup had transformed itself into water under some theoretical bridge, you worked hard to close that chapter and move on. That is a difficult thing to do under the best of circumstances, but what if it was even more trying for you because at this point Bobby had become a public figure whose name and face and business trajectory were hard to avoid? Sure, in this day and age, who doesn't fall into that category? But what if you encountered pictures or references to Bobby so often that it almost seemed like some kind of cruel cosmic joke? For instance, what if everywhere you drove in your very hometown for a couple of months you saw full-sized billboards featuring Bobby beaming down at you? What if this all seemed to culminate that day on the freeway when you found yourself stuck in traffic, inhaling poisonous gas fumes, trapped behind a city bus that was moving at about ten miles an hour, the whole back of which was plastered with such an enormous image of Bobby that it almost looked like he was flattened across your windshield?

But let's say you were made of sterner stuff and gradually learned to tune all this out. "It's just a photo," you might have thought, as you tried to remind yourself of every cheery, up-lifting thing you had ever read on a refrigerator magnet. For example: "Failure provides the opportunity to begin again intelligently" and "Just because you make a mistake doesn't mean you are a mistake." Even though maybe a littler voice in your brain was also muttering at the exact same time, "Yes, but God must be in on this. Bus fumes are so over-the-top symbolic."

But then what if ten, fifteen, twenty more years went by and you got on with your life, went to therapy, pursued your career, owned a lot of dogs, fell in love a bunch of times, and began to feel so healthy emotionally that you could appreci-ate the good part of Bobby again? Maybe this made you feel proud and optimistic, not just about yourself but about man-kind in general and its ability to forgive and to heal. What if you felt so grown-up and balanced and distanced from your own past that one day when someone sent you an announce-ment that Bobby had gotten married, you thought, "How great for Bobby!" But what if, as you were perusing the de-tails of the national press release, you realized that according to the dates Bobby offered, the years you and he had spent "working on the relationship" overlapped exactly with the early dating period of his current relationship? And what if in that moment of comprehension, an odd sucking metaphysical vortex opened up in the center of your handsomely renovated unconscious, and out of it sprung a dendrite-like coiled ap-pendage that vacuumed up the DNA from your positive emotional growth, took all your feelings of goodwill, tum-bled them around in a giant metaphorical reactor, and spit them back out in an emotional tsunami of unpleasantness?

"What the hell is this?" is what you probably thought, even as you did your best to let it pass. Because so what, really? Who gives a shit? It was twenty years ago.

But what if mere weeks after that a big, stupid scandal broke around Bobby, involving assorted charges of infidelity and extortion? And what if the resulting wave of media attention that came in its wake caused all kinds of people to try and drag you back into the maw of Bobby all over again? What if it was big enough that you looked up from your messy desk one day to find a reporter from the *New York Post* and another one from some newspaper in London standing in your driveway? And what if then, in the space of a few days, you were also contacted by *Good Morning America,* the *Today* show, the CBS *Early Show,* and *Nightline,* as well as by individuals from different day parts of CBS and ABC News and assorted magazines, all wanting to talk to you not about whatever you were doing—for example, your new shoe store or haircut salon or the new book you had out or whatever—but instead about Bobby? And what if even when you said no, ABC News called some relative of yours who was completely unconnected to any of this—like, say, a brother who lived in the Midwest—to see if he could shed any light on the whole situation? And then, to top it all off in an orgy of overuse of the fifth letter of the alphabet, what if you also received an email from E! Entertainment Television asking you for an interview and a few pictures from your private collection, to be included in a new show they were doing called *Doomed by Lust?* Yes! What if they really said the show was called *Doomed by Lust?* How did you get connected to a show with a name like that? When did you turn into Charlie Sheen? Or Pamela Anderson? Or a Kar-dashian? Or one of those Housewives of [Name Your City Here]?

And then what if this gossip cycle swelled so much that a few days later, at the checkout counter at the grocery store, you found yourself staring at an endless parade of articles about Bobby with titles like "Inside Bobby's Secret World" and "What Bobby Does to Lure Young Girls"?

Let's say that you're a person who doesn't buy the maga-zines at the grocery checkout line because you honestly don't care who Jennifer Aniston is dating. But still you couldn't help but wonder, "What *does* he do to lure them? Sticky wads of bills attached to invisible wire?" So what if you let your curiosity get the best of you and you decided to pick up one of these magazines and have a look even though it was against your better judgment? And after slogging your way past all those pictures of Jennifer Aniston—in swimwear! in leotards! Oh no! She's crying! Is she going to be okay?—you found an enormous *half-page* picture of *you* with Bobby from twenty-five years ago? And your jaw dropped open because this pic-ture of you, from the early eighties, was right underneath the capitalized word "LURE"? And what if, in that instant, you felt like you had pushed open the door of an occupied public restroom to discover that you were also the person sitting on the toilet in the stall?

"Oh my God!" you heard yourself thinking, or . . . wait, did you just say that out loud? You are suddenly talking more like Jennifer Aniston than you've come to expect. "Are they saying I *lured* someone? Or are they saying I was *lured*?" And what if now you actually wondered, "Was I lured?"

Maybe you were! Think back! Think! Are you involved somehow?

Is it possible that there is another version of you running around somewhere twenty-five years ago over whom you have lost all control?

And then what if you decided to sneak a peek at a different magazine to learn a little more about Jennifer Aniston and also to make sure you aren't in there, too? You're pretty sure the first one was just an aberration. But what if you discover, to your horror, that there is *another* gigantic twenty-five-year-old picture of you with Bobby in this magazine, only this time the article is about how Bobby is leading "a secret double life"? What does this have to do with you? Does that mean you are leading one, too? Have you inadvertently entered one of those other eight dimensions they always speak of in string theory? Could you have possibly tripped on a tear in the fabric of time, where you are now leading a parallel existence that is somehow connected to a secret world of *luring*?

And what if while this was all going on you also started coming in contact with all kinds of information about Bobby and his assorted extracurricular activities from the years that you two were together... information that so totally re-informed and reorganized the way you viewed the landscape of your own past that you wondered if your original theory about the impossibility of combining love and work could have been a mistake? What if the problem wasn't really combining love and work? What if it was combining love and Bobby?

What if now, in your dotage, it finally occurred to you

that all the messages you'd been receiving from the world at large about the best way to be a female in a relationship, which to you has meant placing love on a pedestal that rises above all else, is just a terrible, terrible piece of advice?

That would be a really weird experience to look back on, would it not?

My Advice to the Fidgety Young People

EVERY JUNE, AS I READ OR WATCH EXCERPTS OF THE PITHY, heartfelt speeches delivered by people of note to graduating seniors all across the country, I have to admit: I get a little jealous. So every year I secretly compose the imaginary commencement speech that I would deliver if anyone ever asked. I make it full of timeless wisdom and gallows humor and lace it with enough blunt profanity to hold the attention of and perhaps even inspire the most fidgety audience of young people.

I guess it was a chance to fulfill that fantasy (and a paycheck big enough to cover my mortgage for three months, plus first-class transportation, including airfare and limos) that caused me to say yes to a request to speak at a college career fair in Lafayette, Louisiana, sponsored by a deodorant, a women's magazine, and a line of cosmetics. Not exactly the commencement at Harvard, but my task still sounded noble. As I understood it, I was the lucky person who would dispense, to the idealistic and verbally expressive youth of Lafayette, information and advice about a career in writing.

After several changes of plane, I boarded a tiny aircraft, the only one that landed right in Lafayette itself. I sat next to a salesman who spent the entire flight detailing to our one and only stewardess his thoughts about good and bad ways to die. Happily this leg of the journey was pretty short. About a half hour later, I was greeted at the gate of a very small airport by a ruddy guy who looked as if he ran the refreshment stand at a motocross track. He was dressed in an ensemble that was many shades of shamrock green: bright green slacks, a slightly different green polo shirt, a lighter green sport coat, and somehow a fourth variation on green in a baseball cap. Not that he needed anything additional to tie the outfit together, but each piece was also emblazoned with a logo endorsing a different kind of beer. Turned out he was a rep from the deodorant company that had hired me, so although he looked like he might be sweaty from a morning of racing speedboats, in fact he smelled lemony fresh.

As I followed him to a stretch limo the length of a city block, I decided to climb into the front with him, the better to wrest control of the steering wheel should his morning of sun and suds cause any sudden veering into oncoming traffic.

"Yesterday we had a dude from MTV," he said as we drove out of the terminal parking lot and onto a highway that offered a panoramic view of the many miles of mangrove swamps. "Pretty big turnout. I forget her name. But she was good. She talked about how she dropped out of college after one week because she couldn't find parking. Very inspirational."

"What other events are scheduled for today?" I asked.

"There's a makeover booth. And I heard there's a big astrology tent," he said. "I might stop by later."

While my mind tried to comprehend how this college career fair had incorporated an astrology tent into its prospectus, twenty minutes of silent driving followed. Could it be that astrology was somehow considered a reasonable career path in Lafayette? Was there also going to be a booth for aromatherapy? Would there be a psychic?

But before we headed to the campus, first we stopped by my hotel so I could check in and freshen up a little. My driver/host had allowed an hour for this. Unfortunately most of that time was eaten up at the front desk after I learned there was no record of a reservation in my name. Not until I agreed to put the charges on my personal credit card did everything begin to get back on track.

This left the drive over to the campus as the only time I would have to review my notes. Yes, I had been told by the people who'd hired me that all I needed to do was simply take questions from the audience, but I was planning to end with that. *First,* I would open with the list of things I wanted young writers to know. I would talk to them about the need for telling the truth. I would offer hard-nosed words of solace that they could lean on in tough times . . . words to keep a budding writer from being easily discouraged. I planned to quote Kurt Vonnegut, Jr., on authenticity ("We are what we pretend to be, so we must be careful about what we pretend to be"). I wanted to reference Mark Twain's remarks about editing and rewriting ("A successful book is not made of what is in it, but of what is left out of it").

When the car finally lurched to a stop, I looked up to see the stunned faces of the students by the campus center, staring slack-jawed as the biggest limo in the world tried to park in their student union parking lot. I watched their expressions of great interest turn to painful disappointment before wilting into bewildered contempt when I, not Lady Gaga, emerged from the front, not the back, seat.

"You're speaking in that building over there," my driver said, pointing toward a generic-looking beige brick university building with a small sign pasted on the front that said "Career Fair." As I pushed through the glass doors into a massive, open room that was silent except for the sound of my heels clicking on the expanses of gray linoleum waxed to a super-high-gloss sheen, I was instantly reminded of what they called the "cafetorium" at my grade school. There were the familiar towering stacks of long gray lunch tables, the acoustic-tile ceiling dotted with those lighting fixtures that look like upside-down ice trays. And there were differences as well as similarities. I definitely didn't recall my grade school cafetorium having an enormous cauldron of Soft & Dri deodorant samples underneath a sign that said "Free! Help Yourself!"

Just a few feet beyond the antiperspirant buffet was a specter that still haunts my dreams: rows and rows of molded white plastic chairs, all of them empty.

At the far end of the room was a small stage decorated with an easel that held a blowup of a *Cosmopolitan* cover beneath a banner that said "Soft & Dri." And on the apron of the stage was a bulky gift basket, overflowing with Avon products: moisturizers, cleansers, fragrances, shampoos, conditioners.

A wave of nausea hit as I realized that the basket was for me.

With a half hour to go until my talk, I stood frozen, pretending to read a piece of tourist literature about the area that I'd grabbed from the hotel. It wasn't reassuring to learn that the biggest local attraction anywhere nearby was a medium-sized swamp. By now I was filled with so much anxiety that I was unable to decode the English language, so fixated was I on the thunderous sound of that empty room.

A tiny, hopeful voice inside me spoke up, urging me to relax. "Remember the hectic pace of college life," it said. "Students always show up late for everything!" Then a bigger, darker, smarter voice appeared from somewhere to counter: "Doesn't someone always come early if there's going to be a crowd?"

When at last I heard footsteps, and a lone teenage girl walked in to take a seat in a middle row, I wondered if I should run up to her, embrace her, take her out to buy her dinner and deliver my talk to her over coffee? Or should I simply shake her hand and tell her, "You've gotten your makeover, you've had your chart done. There's not much more I can add. Be sure to grab some free deodorant on your way out! And thanks for showing up!"

"We're going to start in a minute," said my driver, Mr. Bright Green Beer-Logo Ensemble, making a surprise re-appearance as career fair liaison and seminar emcee.

I now counted an audience of eight girls bobbing in that sea of four hundred white chairs. But, I reminded myself, they're not just eight random college girls. They are eight future writers from Lafayette, Louisiana. These are girls who deserve to be treated respectfully and to be encouraged. There could be a young Eudora Welty or Harper Lee among them! Who knows? They might always remember this day.

Summoning a sense of purpose and dignity, I strode to

the front of the room. I would make a difference in these young lives, dammit. I looked into the faces of the students who had come out to hear me. Nothing about them was easy to read. But wasn't that always the case with young people? They were all in their early twenties. That was a time when they were still moldable not yet congealed. They were a group of eight girls who already *knew* that they wanted to write. I hadn't known that about myself when I was their age. I was moved that they were placing themselves in my hands, looking to me to tell them more about the thing they most loved to do. I would not let them down.

"Move your chairs into a circle," I said, dispensing with formality in an attempt to make this career day experience more personal and therefore more memorable. I was now swept up in the idea that the small size of the crowd was actually a blessing. It offered me an opportunity to morph this from a lecture into a seminar. I would zero in on what each of these young writers had on her mind. By giving each of them special attention. I would light a fire under them all that they would never forget. By the time this was over, they would run back to their dorms, crazed with the need to write something that mattered to them. Maybe they would dedicate their future work to me. We would all stay in touch!

"Let's use this time to talk about anything you want," I continued, launching into a few introductory remarks about learning to write in your own voice, and looking at your life in as clear-eyed a way as possible. I offered another Vonnegut quote: "Find a subject you care about and which you feel others should care about. It is this genuine caring, and not your games with language, which will be the most compelling and seductive element in your style." And then, thinking I had gotten the old ball rolling, I turned to address them in earnest.

"What would you guys like to talk about?" I said.

A heavyset girl raised her hand.

"When is the drawing for the Avon basket?" she asked.

Mr. Beer Ensemble raced to the front of the room. Impatiently he grabbed the mike away from her.

"I am not going to announce the winners of the free Avon products and workout videos until *after* Miss Markoe has finished speaking," he boomed. The next time I glanced at the faces of my eight-girl audience, it was with suspicion.

"Are there any other questions?" I asked, still not giving up hope. "Anything I didn't touch on that you would like to discuss?"

"I'd like more information about moisturizers and cleansers," said a second girl.

"Well..." I said, after a beat, as the truth set in. It was time to take my own advice. "I believe it was Mark Twain who said it best: 'Cleanse first, moisturize later.' Anything else?"

No one stirred.

"Okay, then," I said. "Without any further ado, let's get right to that drawing!"

I handed the mike over to our very green emcee. Then I bowed humbly as I got a nice round of applause.

The Dog Prattler

IN THE BEGINNING, LIKE MANY DOG-LOVING AMERICANS, I WAS transfixed by the Dog Whisperer. Between his self-described "calm-assertive manner," his earnest, well-meaning solutions to dog behavioral dilemmas, and his genial, brush-cut good looks, Cesar Millan, host of his own hugely popular dog-training show on the National Geographic Channel, seemed to represent everything smart, sensible, and loving about the human-doggy bond.

I was glued to my set as he backed each new snarling, tooth-baring delinquent canine into a corner, letting them know who was boss with just a few graceful, well-planned moves. I sighed in admiration as he basically saved one dog's life after another by coercing them into rethinking the aggressive behavior they were exhibiting toward the human family who was footing their bills. I cheered as he convinced each dog that it was a win-win situation for them to stop urinating in the bedroom closet. I watched in awe as he glided down the street, on his in–line skates, surrounded by his own personal pack of familiars, none of them pulling him into on–coming traffic or causing him to roll full speed into a tree.

For the whole first season, I looked forward to every new episode of his show, usually watching them more than once. I applauded as Cesar seamlessly blended the best traits of a be–havioral psychologist and an animal rescuer into one affable, preppy-handsome, Ban-Lon shirt–wearing multiculti pack-age.

But by season two, something shifted. Though he wasn't really doing anything differently, I had scrutinized him enough to wonder if, like all big television CEOs, he had ac-cumulated some video mange. His problem-solving tech-niques, though still impressive, had started to feel a little pat and repetitious, maybe a bit suspect.

As I watched Mr. Millan correct each poorly socialized dog by relocating him to the middle of his rehabilitated pack in South Central Los Angeles, confident that "the wisdom of the pack" would transform the problem dog into a better-balanced member of his species, I began to wonder about the recidivism rate after the cameras stopped rolling. How quickly did the dogs revert to their former troublesome ways once they realized that the alpha in the skates wasn't around to dominate them with a full-body rollover anymore?

Time and again I watched as Mr. Millan moved a dog's collar higher up, to a spot just behind the dog's ears, as a cure for the human caretaker's complaints about being yanked along behind the dog during walks like some kind of im-properly weighted racing sled in the Iditarod. In the context of the show, it was nothing short of miraculous the way that collar maneuver instantly transformed the newly enlightened animal from Vin Diesel to Anna Wintour. In a video moment, the once problematic dog would begin strolling languidly beside (and slightly behind) his or her calm-assertive owner.

So after months of struggling with the rude leash manners of my dog, Hedda, I decided to give his method a try. I followed Mr. Millan's advice and slid Hedda's collar up behind her ears. And behold: it worked! But only because she was now uncomfortable and puzzled. After about ten minutes of tiptoeing beside and slightly ahead of the oddly subdued, overly upright, and lightly choking Hedda, I decided that this version of a walk with her was exactly the same amount of fun as accompanying a postoperative patient and their mobile IV unit on a stroll down the hospital hall the day after gallbladder surgery. In other words, it was about half as exhilarating as it had been when she was out of control and barreling down the street, filled with such an uncontainable amount of joie de vivre that she was pulling me like a water-skier. At least the old style of walk let me derive vicarious thrills from watching a creature in the throes of unbridled gleeful interest in *everything*.

Then I started thinking about how part of the fun of hanging out with another species is, for me, readjusting my eyes to see the world as they do. Every day during the serving of breakfast, when one of my dogs becomes so excited that she rears up on her hind legs and walks backward into a table, I marvel anew at how deep her excitement is in that moment. I am impressed by how much she loves eating (while also astounded by what an unbelievable pinhead she is to not know that the table is going to be there again the next day).

Sure, I could insist that she and all my other dogs sit quietly at attention while I display for them my considerable breakfast preparation skills. (And they are considerable. I believe my homemade "dog loaf" is the finest in the land.) My guess is that Mr. Millan and his staff probably require rapt attentiveness every time they make an appearance in front of the group. Yes, it would eliminate all the moaning and the pawing at the backs of my legs. But my dogs' authentic responses amuse me. And I'm pretty sure that the divot in my calf will heal in time.

Eventually I started wondering, Who exactly *is* this Mr. Know-It-All Dog Whisperer, anyway? And why am I taking his advice while he is ignoring mine?

A little research* revealed no university-sanctioned credentials or important government titles or grants. Just a self-taught guy who, since childhood in his native Mexico, seemed to have such a "remarkable rapport with dogs" that he was given the nickname *El Perrero,* "the dog boy."

Damn! I said to myself. That is not all that impressive. Plenty of people think that I, too, have remarkable rapport with dogs. And there are other parallels: I have no credentials or grants. Plus, oddly enough, my childhood nickname was *El Perrero Que Tiene una Vagina,* even though I spent my early childhood in New Jersey. What's to keep me from calling myself an expert and getting a show? After all, it only makes good sense! How many times have I adopted an abused, unwanted creature from a shelter and transformed him into a cherished, beloved family member? How often have I turned an insecure, starving beast into one who is so smug and overfed that he offers me no choice but to sleep in a tight little ball way over in one corner of the bed?

---

*And when I say *little,* I am not kidding. I looked him up on Wikipedia.

Answer: Plenty of times! And I have the chiropractor bills to prove it! Sometimes the creature has even been a dog!

Then it occurred to me: The first step is to start my own dog-training school!

Yes! I can do it! I too have a method to share! After all, who's going to stop me? The bottom line is that any advice taken from any dog guru . . . be it the Dog Whisperer, the kid who works at Petco, or me . . . is an act of blind faith. It's a lot like buying vitamins, or believing the praise of a salesperson who tells you that, yes, you absolutely look beautiful in that bathing suit. By the time you find out that the service provided was mainly a lie, it's not worth the stress it would take to bother getting a refund.

Because let's face it: when we hire an animal-behavior mentor, we are buying their invented vision of the human-animal bond. In almost every case, they made it all up. No member of the other species in question was actually consulted. Often no research, beyond firsthand observation, was even done. It's a little like choosing a religion: you take a look at the holidays, then pick the one that will make your life better, not worse.

Naturally, a visit to my dog ranch to study my method of Flexible Cohabitation (patent pending) will afford a very different set of insights than a visit to the Cesar Millan Dog Psychology Center. It's all a question of what set of rationalizations you are willing to buy. Ask yourself: Do you want a dog who will walk behind you and obey your every command? Or do you want a more casual, improvisational, fun-filled human-dog bond? If your answer to the second question is YES!, then read on.

By using my method, and rejecting the methods of Mr.

Millan, you will find that both the human and the dog will experience less stress. And the truth is that the more you accept your dog for who he is and not try to mold him into what you expect him to be, the more you will also accept yourself. At least that's what I like to tell people who are vacillating about writing me a check because they are not so sure I know what I'm talking about.

FLEXIBLE COHABITATION
(Patent Pending)
My Dog-Care Plan for YOU

FAQ

Q. How do I know if Flexible Cohabitation (patent pending) is right for me?

A. Well, let me ask you this: Do you have the patience and follow-through necessary to work with your dog for an hour a day, every day, for months, even years on end? Do you want to endure the tedium and discomfort of repeatedly giving your well-intentioned, sad-eyed pet forceful commands that make them feel manipulated and unhappy while at the same time making you feel tyrannical? If you answered, "Will the program still work if I only do it once a week?" then I believe that Flexible Cohabitation is the plan for you. With Flexible Cohabitation, all that's required is that you sit back in your favorite chair with the icy-cold beverage of your choice and enjoy life's rich pageantry as it unfolds before you. Because unlike Cesar Millan, I was not raised a member of the male gender in the macho culture of Mexico, and therefore I am not inclined to ask my human clients to subject themselves to painful puncture wounds by performing an alpha rollover when their dog appears dangerous or aggressive. Instead, with Flexible Cohabitation, I will show you how to enjoy a meaningful human-dog bond anyway, while allowing the dog you love so dearly to behave exactly as he or she wishes.

Q. You can't mean that you are advocating letting dogs run all higgledy-piggledy through your home?

A. To this I reply, "Obviously you have never been to my home."

With Flexible Cohabitation, I will share with you my very special form of Zen nonattachment to material goods, which, in these days of economic turmoil, your bank account is going to love! I wish I had known you back in the days when I had my blue pin-striped sofa, which was so full of holes from dogs circling and getting comfortable that the stuffing was pouring out of it in at least six different places. With my method, your life will be free from worries about how to get unusual stains off delicate upholstery. Gone are the days of wandering around with a spray bottle of Windex and a chamois, trying to remove smeary noseprints from gleaming reflective surfaces! In fact, no more delicate upholstery! No more gleaming reflective surfaces! Period!

Q. Will I have to employ terrifying, guilt-inducing accessories like an electrified fence and collar?

A. Not only will you never again have the need for so much as a choke chain, but I will show you how to make yourself believe that tugging on a rope toy is in itself a form of aerobic exercise that helps to shape and tone your calves, thighs, biceps, and abdominals while improving your dog's physique as well. I will even offer easy diagrams to help you convince yourself of this!

And that's not all!

With Flexible Cohabitation, I will help you feel good about the tendency you already have to give your dog full access to your plate at mealtimes by showing you how it can help you cut down on thousands of calories a day!

You'll be amazed at how much more free time you have when you abandon the tedium of traditional dog training and accept living alongside your dog in the harmony and chaos that nature intended! And when all is said and done, you will find that they love you exactly the same amount!

Q. What about tooth brushing? Do I have to brush my dog's teeth on your plan?

A. No. My guarantee to you, the consumer: With Flexible Cohabitation, you don't even have to brush your own teeth. And you will go to sleep at night knowing that 100 percent of your money will be spent not just to build a long-dreamed-of addition to my house but also to pay for the high-end canned food and vitamins to which my own dogs have unfortunately become accustomed. (Offer void where prohibited by law.)

Q. Isn't the relationship you are recommending here the kind of doormat relationship that you commonly rail against among human beings?

A. No! Not in the least! Because in this case . . . well, okay . . . yes. In a way it is. But with Flexible Cohabitation, since the relationship in question is with a dog, it's so much more appealing. Gone are the power struggles involving appropriate roles, the painful arguments full of humiliating personal insults. Gone are the gut-wrenching lawsuits over property and children. Now, at last, you are truly free to work out your troubling childhood issues with nothing more at stake than a few sofa cushions, some socks, and the occasional rug.

Virginity Entrepreneurs

COME WITH ME NOW, IF YOU CAN STAND IT FOR A THEORETICAL second, back to those golden-hued days of a minute ago when George W. Bush, our dunderheaded former president, hadn't yet announced the total collapse of the global economy and Barack Obama was but a hope-filled gleam in a potential voter's eye. Come with me back to a time when a seemingly normal girl in her early twenties, after giving herself the pop-starry pseudonym of Natalie Dylan, publicly announced her intention to auction off her virginity on eBay and use the profits to finance her college education. This may have seemed like just one more offbeat listing for eBay shoppers used to bidding on "4 sets of 3 unused mortuary toe tags" or "Debra Winger's childhood doll," but it was new to me. It was my first encounter with the unsettling vocation of the self-employed virginity entrepreneur.

The idea had apparently gotten rolling a few years earlier in Europe when a lesbian student at the University of Bristol sold her virginity online for £8,400. The next recorded case was in 2007 when a young British physics student at the University of Salford was offered a cool ten thousand pounds by a potential deflowerer. After that Natalie Dylan followed suit, becoming the first American to ride a winning horse in this particular derby. And once her story hit the throbbing jugular vein of Internet sensationalism, her auction price climbed up over a million dollars.

Perfect, I thought as I sat in front of my computer, peering down from my wobbly perch in middle age at what appeared to be a disturbing new trend. *Just what our culture was missing: another talent-free route to fame and riches through self-exploitation!* As I began to drown in alarming visions of what it would feel like to be a young woman who had set herself up for an intimate encounter with some unsavory ne'er-do-well, I also started scrutinizing the barrage of quotes from the eerily articulate Ms. Dylan. Her words were more rational than I'd expected, which made me even more uncomfortable.

"Like most little girls, I was raised to believe that virginity is a sacred gift a woman should reserve for just the right man," she said to an interviewer at the time. "For me, valuing virginity as sacred is simply not a concept I could embrace. But valuing virginity monetarily—now that's a concept I could definitely get behind."

Since the beginning of recorded history, civilizations in all parts of the world have assigned immense immeasurable and mystical worth to virginity. The vestal virgins of ancient Rome were thought to wield such otherworldly powers that a condemned criminal needed only to accidentally lay eyes on one during his march to the gallows in order to have his life spared. Joan of Arc's vow of virginity at fourteen was so highly regarded by God that He chose her to lead France in battle against England in the Hundred Years War. (Okay, yes, this was according to the voices in her head. Then again, we all know the bio of the woman God is said to have picked to become the mother of His kid.)

Even today, all these years later, having had sex remains one of the few things a young woman gets status points for *not* accomplishing. She will never, for example, get the same praise and positive reinforcement for not graduating from high school, not losing weight, or not learning to cook. Her window of opportunity for collecting rewards for her sex-free life remains very specific, however. The mystical powers ascribed to her purity have never been thought to grow stronger with age. Even back in 700 B.C., a vestal virgin who was recruited at the age of ten was out of a job permanently by the time she hit thirty. (On the plus side, at least in ancient times older virgins could all breathe a sigh of relief when decisions were being made about who to throw into a volcano.)

"Why buy the cow when you can get the milk for free?" is one of those ridiculous homilies I remember hearing as a kid. It was, I suppose, a way for adults to scare hormonally charged girls like me into keeping their underwear on. But it never made sense to me because . . . were my friends and I supposed to be the cows in that scenario? I'd never thought of myself as a cow. Then again, it had never occurred to me to think of a cow as the CEO of a small milk-distribution center.

Considering how hard it always has been to get a good job right out of high school, to say nothing of how ridiculous tuition and interest rates on student loans have become, I could certainly see how this virginity-entrepreneur idea might begin to snowball. And so, of course, in the last couple years a teenager in Germany closed a deal for $13,000, and a New Zealander who called herself Unigirl aced the full $32,000 she needed for college tuition.

Contemplating this whole notion on the one hand made me queasy, while on the other it left me marveling at the improved level of self-esteem among these young girls relative to my own at that age. Because as coldly calculating, reckless, and unromantic as they appeared to be, my own loss-of-virginity story seemed, in retrospect, a lot more disturbing.

Natalie Dylan, Unigirl, and their fellow virginity saleswomen were the granddaughters of the sexual revolution, raised in the era of personal branding. This enabled them to view their various abilities as commodities worth a tidy sum. Whereas I, who grew up an interested but not too active soldier at the dawn of that revolution itself, could only see my own virginity as an embarrassing symbol of all the things I lacked. To me, virginity was something to be gotten rid of quickly, then never discussed again, like body odor or a bad haircut.

From my uncomfortable spot on the sidelines at eighth-grade make-out parties, where I stood cracking jokes by the refreshment table, trying not to eat too many chips while watching with envy as the other girls disappeared into dark corners or back rooms with the boys I liked, I could see no evidence of the thing my mother called "dating." The way she'd explained it, "dating" was something that happened when large groups of neatly dressed, benignly chuckling teens, wholly uninterested in the notion of two genders, gathered in brightly lit community rec rooms to enjoy soft drinks and pound cake—although, even in this cake-filled scenario, one had to be constantly on guard to keep from getting hijacked into a world of fallopian tubes, sperm, and the horrors of pregnancy. I was never clear on whether the pound cake she promised was served before the pregnancy stuff or after.

By high school, in the late sixties, my family had moved three thousand miles, from North Miami to a hilly, tree-lined suburb on the San Francisco Peninsula, where I quickly learned, like every transfer student trying to assimilate into a brand-new high school social order, that status and group membership had been decided long before I'd arrived. The "in" crowd had apparently stopped taking applications somewhere around third grade. But since the "weird arty kids" were still accepting new members, I took a deep breath, stopped setting my hair, and started wearing dark eyeliner.

Yet, even out here on the West Coast, happily surrounded by my brand-new circle of baby artists, I was still unable to catch a glimpse of that brightly lit dating scenario my mother was selling. On the other hand, little by little I was getting a tantalizing glimpse of a truly compelling erotic subculture full of music and sexual innuendo erupting in all the dark corners around me.

In addition to the Beatles, the Rolling Stones, the Zombies, and the Yardbirds—with whom I'd had many hours' worth of deep, meaningful imaginary liaisons—there were suddenly all kinds of seductive-looking, long-haired local San Francisco bands with cryptic, inscrutable names that I could ogle in person. All I needed to do was get permission to take the bus into the city and I could immerse myself in crowds of oddly dressed young people who were smoking, tripping, and passing around enormous bottles of wine. Not only was no one checking IDs, but as long as I changed into the wide-brimmed hat and magenta midcalf-length suede coat I'd bought at the Salvation Army sometime before the bus ride was over, I could transform myself from a bland high school sophomore into someone mysterious who seemed to fit right in.

No, I wasn't welcomed back into the home of my tidy, shiny parents dressed in that outfit. My dad, in his jaunty Arnold Palmer golf hats and pressed shirts and slacks, commented more than once, as I became increasingly whimsical with all my clothing choices, that he thought I looked like a circus clown. Oddly enough, that was not the look he had in mind for his daughter. It was also not the look I felt I'd achieved. He would have died if he'd ever heard about the afternoon when a woman who was wearing three overcoats and a pair of tennis shoes so threadbare they were held together by rubber bands came up to me as I was walking toward the San Francisco bus depot, made an empathetic face, and pressed a Hershey bar with almonds into my hands.

"Because I understand," she'd said as she smiled sweetly and walked away.

When I opened the outer wrapper, I saw that she had hidden a five-dollar bill inside. Naturally, I was a little alarmed to learn that I looked like a worst-case scenario to an actual homeless person.

Nevertheless, every weekend I could get away with it, I would go into San Francisco with any of my new friends who were available and spend long, satisfying days being jostled at street fairs, poked and prodded at concerts, my ears ringing from blaring amps, my eyes stinging from billowing clouds of secondhand smoke. Then I would stumble home, tired and happy, right before my curfew, resplendent in brand-new, hand-strung beaded necklaces and earrings (which would usually break by the end of the week), my arms laden with illegible psychedelic posters full of foul language and current editions of *Zap Comix*. With barely a nod to my parents, I would repair to my room, where I would light cinnamon candles, take out my Rapidograph pen, and copy the ink drawings by R. Crumb and Rick Griffin and Victor Moscoso, trying to match their shading and cross-hatching as I duplicated their dancing peanuts in top hats and drooling, perspiring, bug-eyed lunatic people. These were like images beamed to me from a funnier if slightly incomprehensible dimension not too far away that I hoped to someday inhabit.

Meanwhile, in a parallel universe that was still sharing a roof with my own, my parents were drowning in television and newspaper stories full of ominous warnings about drug use, sex, and disease among people my age. They saw my destiny forever ruined by hallucinogen-induced brain damage and unwanted love-in babies. And although I'd never so much as smoked a joint, as far as my parents could tell, I was right on the verge of being lost forever in the quicksand of heroin addiction.

"The only thing I ask of you," my mother said during one particularly hysterical rant, which began after she read an issue of *Life* magazine about the growing popularity of cohabitation, "is that you never live with someone and not be married."

In that one breath she not only mapped the course for my entire adulthood but also destroyed her own credibility, by having repeatedly "asked" many things of me even earlier that very day.

As time went on, my parents became increasingly paranoid. Everything I said or did seemed, to my mother, like an early warning sign of some kind of substance abuse. But the more my father used the phrase "beardo weirdo" to describe someone I had a crush on, the more I knew I was on exactly the right track. If they were against what I was doing, then I was for it. Whatever "it" was.

Although I had never done any of the things my parents feared, the way I saw it, my life with them was its own hellish torment. So the more they lectured me about drugs and pregnancy and VD, the more I resolved to prove them wrong. They didn't know me. They would *never* know me. And the more they claimed to know me, the wronger they would be.

Therefore I turned my back on sex and drugs and decided to remain a virgin. This put me at cross-purposes with my carefully cultivated new image as a budding artistic visionary, dressed in purple and swathed in enigmatic beaded artifacts from San Francisco.

The irony was not totally lost on me. I worried constantly that the lack of sex, drugs, and depravity in my life was going to jeopardize my future as an artist. After all, the kind of unconventional rock-and-roll free spirit I was using as my model embraced all the things I was now rejecting. "I wonder if someone can come from a background like mine and still be a creative person?" I fretted in my diary during my junior year of high school. "Sometimes I look at my life and I say, No, Merrill...you can never become anything special. Why? Because you don't fit the pattern of successful people. Look at your family. No one else in your boring normal life exhibits any great talent. Today I read about John Lennon and his precocious adolescent sex life and I thought, 'I probably need to have a real love affair in order to become a real artist.'"

What was a girl to do?

My short-term plan was to continue to affect an air of jaded world-weariness and count on improper assumptions about me being made from the company I kept: a group of artistic kids—many of whom had already been busted for drugs, and most of whom were far more sexually experienced than I. So I kept my fingers crossed that, until I left home, I would benefit from guilt by association.

By the time I got to college, I had come to view my virginity as categorical proof that I was nothing more than an uninspired cog in the wheel of a system I was supposed to be helping to overthrow. If I didn't jump in and play the game of life as it was meant to be played, I would get drummed right out of the art world before my first show. So losing my virginity rocketed to the top of my first-quarter short list of Things to Do.

There was one problem: I didn't have a boyfriend. I'd broken up with the poor guy I'd been tormenting during my senior year in high school, and now I didn't know anyone at all.

Then one afternoon, a week or two in, I took the bus by myself to an art show off campus. This wasn't intended as an expedition to ferret out boyfriend candidates; I was mainly excited about the possibilities of going places by myself without first having to bust through a roadblock of parents with curled lips and raised eyebrows. What a relief it was not to have to explain to anyone when I would be back.

The art show was held in a communal house that had been rented by a group of grad students. It didn't look like any art show I'd been to before: large, unframed airbrushed paintings with staples sticking out of gessoed edges hung on the dirty walls of a living room so underfurnished its occupants appeared to have been recently evicted. To me this meant only one thing: the people living there were too smart to get hung up on mundane middle-class bullshit like furniture. Why bother with chairs and end tables if you had a dozen photo-realist paintings of pasty bourgeois people floating in swimming pools?

When I walked in, wearing my navy peacoat and my green felt hat with the leopard-print band, a couple of guys my age immediately began to circle me. The first one had followed me in from the bus stop. He wasn't bad-looking: curly brown afro, Benjamin Franklin glasses, a blue work shirt. But he was quickly disqualified for appearing to be a little *too* happy to meet me. He smiled too much, he was too familiar, too touchy-feely. In a flash I could visualize this overly enthusiastic, far too ardent stranger whaling away on top of me, grimacing and thrashing as he expelled giants bullets of sweat like a drawing by S. Clay Wilson. The second guy had long blondish hair, wide-wale corduroy pants, and suede cowboy boots. As superficial signifiers went, this was a hat trick. More important, he was aloof, with an edge that seemed somehow threatening. That he was an upperclassman art major from my very department *and* willing to talk to me made me feel like an insider!

I didn't think he was "cute" per se; he was smallish, skinny, and sort of pigeon-chested. But from my perspective, he loomed much larger, held aloft by the immensity of his arrogant disregard for everything. That frosty, unpleasant air of his told me that he was a person of high standards. We had all let him down. Hopefully I would prove the rare exception.

I began following him around the exhibit like an orphaned baby duck, noting how he rolled his eyes at the same paintings that had minutes before impressed me with their details and airbrush techniques.

"This is bullshit," he said, with a sweeping hand gesture that applied across the board. "Guy's an asshole. A punk."

I nodded my head in deference.

From that point on, I tried to make all my comments both vague and dismissive, in the hopes that if they were wrong, they might still seem to contain a hidden, much smarter second meaning.

His name was Brad, and he was so thoroughly unimpressed by the art in this exhibit that he was ready to leave the moment he arrived. "Go get a hot dog?" he asked, tilting his head toward the door before completing even one full lap around the room. I nodded and tagged along behind him as he headed down the block. At first I was a little bit concerned because I was a vegetarian. But it turned out that this dietary restriction of mine was less of a problem than I'd anticipated since at no point did Brad offer to buy me any food. Instead I stood beside him in the small chalet-style fast-food establishment and watched him pile assorted condiments onto his hot dog before he consumed it.

Afterward we both climbed into the cabin of his truck. A pickup truck! How completely perfect was that?

Brad explained that he might as well give me a ride back to his apartment since he lived across the street from the bus stop I would be using. No mention was ever made of giving me a ride back to my dorm.

This notable lack of old-world hospitality didn't prevent me from saying yes to an invitation to come inside and see his work. Sure, I knew I was taking a risk going into the apartment of a stranger, but I was dazzled by the fact that he *had* an apartment. Everything in it was *his*. The chairs were *his*. The food in the refrigerator: *his!* He paid his own bills. He had his own truck. What didn't this guy have?

And what an apartment! Although it was only a three-room flat at the back of a multifamily classic Berkeley brown-shingle house, its central room was dominated by a real restaurant counter, purchased at a thrift store, with four red leather stainless steel stools and a Formica top. Whatever Brad lacked in charm, he made up for with his very own real-life version of Edward Hopper's *Nighthawks!* Take that, Mom and Dad! No more molded plastic dinette sets in my brave new world! Since you saw me a month ago, I have *totally changed*. Now I live life in the kind of vivid 3D realm neither of you could even imagine, let alone handle.

It only took a couple of minutes inside Brad's apartment for me to notice an uptick in uncomfortable silences. But more than likely, they were my fault. I was young and inexperienced. And anyway, it made sense that Brad wasn't verbal. He was an artist. Words were not his thing. I couldn't wait to see his paintings. His disrespect for the work of others told me that a door was about to be opened and I would inhale the icy clean air of pure insight. Which is why I was so surprised that he had only two paintings to show me. And those paintings were... well, I wasn't sure what they were. They were kind of hastily executed knockoffs of ancient Near Eastern erotica onto which Brad had collaged a border of glitter, sequins, and plastic doll heads. Now my challenge was figuring out what expression to put on my face as I looked at them, in order to best reflect a sophisticated level of appreciation I didn't feel.

"They're *supposed* to be bad," Brad explained, when I remained silent. "They're intentionally bad."

That caught me off guard. I'd never heard of anyone doing anything like that. But now that he'd said it, I could see how that might be the kind of interesting choice a real artist might make. Still, I didn't get why he hadn't done them just a little bit better. Or a whole lot worse. But then again, I was the idiot who didn't always understand what Bob Dylan was saying.

"Great. Really great." I smiled and then just kept on nodding.

Looking back, I wonder if there was anything Brad could have done right then to turn me off. If he'd been Jeffrey Dahmer I probably would have rationalized the severed heads and penises in his refrigerator with a simple "Well, they needed refrigeration. Where else was he going to put them?" The truth was, Brad's indifference and lack of consideration only inspired me.

Even though I'd only been living in Berkeley for a few weeks, I had begun to adjust to perplexing encounters with the opposite sex. First there was the guy who followed me back to my dorm and read me his free-form erotic poetry until I said I had to go inside and do my homework, at which point he got mad and accused me of not listening to my own body. Then there was the guy who came up to me on the steps of Sproul Hall while I was petting a dog. "How come you'll give all that love to a stray dog but you won't give me any?" he asked repeatedly, more or less daring me to give the wrong answer. Later, I actually thought about what he'd said because, after all, this was college so it couldn't be as stupid as it sounded, could it? Finally there was the guy who, perhaps after reading too many fake *Penthouse* letters supposedly written by "college coeds," followed me down the street and into a bookstore. "I'd really like to fuck you," he said, apropos of nothing, scaring me so badly that I took off running in the other direction. As unnerving as that had been, I still proudly chalked the whole weird incident up to my new grittier life full of authentic real-world experiences in the urban jungle. I now lived in a town full of men and women who weren't ashamed to crave sex. We didn't mess with brightly lit rooms full of soft drinks and pound cake here in Berkeley. No more plastic suburbia to numb me now. Here at last were crucial milestones logged on the road to making real art.

So, at the end of the evening of the day I met Brad and his intentionally bad paintings, I climbed onto a mattress on top of a loft he'd built behind his *Nighthawks* diner and made out with him. Up to this point, I had made out with only two people in my life, total. It had taken my high school senior year boyfriend a full year of earnest love letters to get to second base.

"I'm still a virgin," I said to Brad.

"Really?" he said, oddly indignant. "Then you better go to Planned Parenthood and get on the pill." He rolled off me, grabbed a pad of paper and a pen, and scribbled detailed instructions on transferring from one bus line to another to get to the clinic in Oakland. His message was clear: if I expected to spend more time with him, everything about me had to change.

As I rode the bus back to my dorm, I ruminated on the events of the day, attempting to reinterpret them so they were more to my liking. Was Brad letting me know, in his terse impatient way, that he liked me so much he couldn't bear to wait? Was it possible that once I gave in and played along, we would be magically transformed into one of those great artist couples, like whoever that lady was and Picasso?

I didn't see or hear from Brad again until a few nights later, when we decided to get together for what amounted to our first date. When we spoke on the phone, that trip to Planned Parenthood remained the number one topic. So even though I had a lot of schoolwork to do, I resigned myself to making the cross-town trip. Because, come on: my schedule needed to be flexible enough to accommodate important life-changing events. Same way I had managed to make room for that day-long Black Power conference, where I was the only representative of my gender and race; I went because I knew that it was culturally important for me to attend. And in a different way, so was this. Anyway, I didn't feel like I had a choice. Even though if, just a few months before, my parents had given me a bunch of orders involving bus trips and pills, I would have stormed out of the room, now I was behaving like someone who'd been abducted and imprisoned in a basement for a decade and had developed Stockholm syndrome.

In the indie film version of this story, it would probably

be time for a "love montage." This one would begin with a tracking shot of a small art-house revival theater, where we would find my character standing behind Brad in a movie line, waiting to pay for her own ticket. Then it would follow her as she followed him up to the snack bar, where we would watch her digging around in her big leather purse, hoping to find enough loose change to buy herself a popcorn. Cut to the inside of the theater itself, where, on the smallish screen, W. C. Fields would be shaving a man in a barber chair before the camera panned over to the audience. There, with the movie light flickering gently on their faces, my character and her date would be sitting side by side, not even acknowledging each other. Next would come a series of quick shots of the two of them driving away in his truck, still not touching or saying a word. Then, from a camera angle at the bottom of a stairwell, we would bear silent witness as they quietly marched up to his flat at the back of the house, hearing only the sound of their shoes scuffling on the rotted wood as they climbed.

The montage would end with one of those uncomfortably clear overhead shots of my character lying flat on her back, open-eyed, as she lost her virginity.

This would be a tricky scene to direct because it would somehow need to visually convey how mechanically Brad made what I don't think you could really call love: how he moved like an alien who had never experienced what the earthlings called "emotions." How he touched like an animatronic statue, perhaps Abe Lincoln on Main Street in Disneyland or one of the mechanized Santa's helpers from the Macy's Christmas window display.

Throughout the several minutes of the actual event, things

were far too quiet. I knew I should be making gasping noises of some kind, but I didn't dare try because I wasn't sure how a real-life version of these noises needed to sound. So at the very juncture where Natalie Dylan was probably fantasizing about how much of her windfall she would spend on an amazing new back-to-school wardrobe, I was lying there embarrassed and disoriented, not even sure if the whole thing had officially ended.

Had it gone badly?

Had it gone well?

On what basis was this experience supposed to be evaluated?

When Brad rolled off me this time, I figured I'd better follow his lead. After all, it was his house. So when he got dressed, I got dressed too. That I couldn't think of anything to say only matched the fact that neither could he. Clearly I had done something wrong. Why else would he be acting so cold and aloof?

It was then that I noticed that there was blood on the sheets. I had either started my period or it had been Mission Accomplished. In either case, I felt bad about causing him an extra trip to the Laundromat. So I apologized as he wordlessly stripped the sheets off the bed. Then we stood around for a few minutes while he made some coffee. After that he walked me to the bus stop and left me there to wait.

Sitting alone on a cracked green Naugahyde bus seat, headed back to my dorm, I stared out the window and watched the streets of Berkeley go by. Where, I wondered, was the emotional center in this for me? I didn't feel anything. I didn't have a sense of accomplishment. But mostly, I was unable to decipher what all the fuss was about. What was

·it about sex that people liked so much? A million musicians, a million writers, a million paintings and poems and stories and songs, all rendered completely incomprehensible. I'd always thought that when I arrived at this moment, the magic they were all describing would be revealed. Had it been, but I missed it? Or was sex one of those things that everyone else agreed was great but I would never understand, like, say, orange Slurpees or Red Skelton? What part of what had just happened was supposed to have been the good part?

Here's what else was weird: in all my meandering thoughts during what might have been my moments of basking in the afterglow, as the bus made its way down College Avenue toward my dorm, I never once wondered if I should have waited for the right guy to come along. Like Natalie Dylan, I had turned my back on acting like one of those naïve teenagers who bought into that romantic crap. Those myths were for people who weren't part of the solution because they were part of the problem.

Yet unlike Natalie Dylan, who'd said she was seeking "a combination of a great time with a good connection and a financial agreement that I can be happy with," I had asked for nothing from anyone and had succeeded one hundred percent.

So puzzled was I by what had or had not just happened sexually that a couple of weeks later I went back for seconds to clear a few things up. Maybe some circuit would light this time, now that I knew what to expect? At the very least, a second visit would allow me to amortize the cost of my new birth control pills down to just pennies a serving.

Unfortunately, nothing that happened the second time—

or the truly unnecessary third time—taught me anything more about sex or human relations, except that I could accurately predict each of Brad's moves in his never-changing sequence, based on the one that had preceded it.

By winter quarter, I was seeing Brad only intermittently. The awkward silences were wearing me down. And after he decided it was a good idea to introduce me to several other girls with whom he was also sleeping, I finally threw in the towel. And by "the towel," I am referring to my search for an actual reason to continue our loose association. Especially after that night of watching him take PCP and throw his television set out the window. I guess I had hoped that if we saw each other for a while, something meaningful would have no choice but to develop. Wasn't that the way the world worked? Any seed that was planted, when offered the right amount of water and sun, had to grow into something or other, right?

Looking back, I marvel at the way the teenage me made choices. I wonder, too, which part of our schizophrenic culture might be held responsible for making young female humans require less from their courtship rituals than do sea turtles or millipedes. In all of the animal kingdom, only delusional teenage human girls steeped in their own melancholia seem to require no special acrobatic nest-building competitions or intricate mating dances involving red inflatable bladders to be convinced of the worth of a suitor. Why bother with dangerous hormone-driven treks across the Arctic wasteland, like the ones Mother Nature requires for male penguins and moose, when a scowling, anorexic, paintbrush-holding guy with an outsized sense of his own importance gets the same results simply by being rude?

Which brings me back to Natalie Dylan and her fellow virginity entrepreneurs, with their sleazy online auctions and fat bank accounts. Tawdry though their deeds may have been, at least they could logically explain their own motives. At least they held themselves in such high regard that they looked at the chance for someone else to spend time with them as a high-ticket item. The best I could do was imagine myself as the provider of raw data for a sociology experiment no one was conducting.

The truth is, if a Web auction had been available to me back in my Berkeley years, even the greasiest, most debauched bidder would have been demonstrating more appreciation for me than the rude little art scenester I picked. And even if I'd been hanging out with friends like Natalie Dylan, I'd probably still have thrown my virginity in as a bonus to the highest bidder in a separate auction of my used textbooks. I simply didn't have the ego to be a self-employed capitalist, let alone an underpaid volunteer escort.

That's why the modern-day horror stories about teenage girls and their sexting and hooking-up activities don't surprise me so much as they make me feel sad. The only thing girls are doing now that is demonstrably worse than what I did at their age is starting younger, thereby entitling themselves to even more years of hysterical late-night phone calls to like-minded girlfriends in which they will endlessly rehash and analyze the incomprehensible results of their bad love decisions. Decisions, I must add, that are made without the benefit of a fully wired frontal lobe. Because recent neurological research now explains what I could never have known: that it's no accident that teenagers are devoted to being boneheads. The frontal lobes of the brain, the area that allows us to comprehend the idea of actions having consequences, aren't finished being wired for functioning until your late twenties. If ever a religious philosopher or moralist needed a place to anchor cautionary advice about waiting until you're twenty-eight to pick partners or marry, that frontal lobe data would be a good place to start.

But the worst part is that if I'd known this handy fact back when I was in college, it probably wouldn't have changed the course of my behavior very much. After all, the teenage version of me would have thought the very idea of worrying about consequences before you act was excessively "middle-class." I would have argued that no great artist ever worried about consequences. And I would have been processing all of this with only a partially wired frontal lobe.

How to Spot an Asshole

I WAS IN THE SHOWER WHEN I HEARD THE PHONE RING AND THE answering machine pick up. Over the whoosh of the running water, I could just make out a deep, flat voice leaving a lengthy message. Concerned that some kind of an emergency was unfolding, I wrapped myself in a towel and stood dripping wet in the hallway to hear the details. It scared me that I didn't recognize the voice. Was it a wrong number? A dangerous interloper? When he hung up, I played the whole thing back.

Slowly it dawned on me that the voice belonged to a guy I had met a few nights before at a dinner party. Apparently he had gotten my number from mutual friends and decided to call. The content of the message, when I boiled it all down, was basically that he thought it would be a good idea for us to spend some time together. Nothing scary there.

The bloodcurdling part, however, was in the way he chose to express that thought to me. Here is the actual transcript:

"Hello, Merrill? I'd like to see you sometime, the earlier the better. Right now would be perfect. If you're in the mood to do something tonight, that would be good. Because my moods shift so dramatically these days that it's easier for me to go on impulse than to make a date with someone and then realize when the time comes that I am not really in the mood to do anything. So that's kind of the way I want to operate."

He might as well have said: "Hey, Merrill...if you have a ton of free time and would like to babysit a self-absorbed, needy, demanding middle-aged adult who is only interested in using you as a sounding board for his neurotic problems, you can look long and hard but I doubt you'll find anyone better than me."

His words were immediately filed for posterity in my very special pantheon of unintentionally revealing statements, right next to those of the seemingly nice woman I met at a job who told me that she spoke with her shrink every day on the phone and then went on to ask, "Can I have your phone number? I love to talk on the phone, but I wore a lot of my old friends out."

One of the prime achievements of my adult life, right up there with owning my own washer and dryer, has been learning to read the warning signs broadcast by an asshole. With all the social networking going on, the importance of watching and listening for pernicious symptoms when you first meet someone is more important than ever, because these days the lines have become so blurred that it's easy to find out you are "friends" with all kinds of people you simply have no reason to trust, beyond a stated appreciation of Radiohead.

Somewhere between our Neanderthal beginnings and the twenty-first century, the instructional software that was supposed to be installed in each of us to teach us how to connect with appropriate members of our species for the purposes of mating seems to have been infected with some kind of virus. Every other species on planet Earth received their behavioral software, plus tutorials. Take the buff-breasted sandpiper male, for example, who arrives straight from the manufacturer knowing how to flash the undersides of his wings and make those special clucking sounds that magnetize the female and fill her with lust. Or the male porcupine, who somehow understands, despite unfavorable odds, how to successfully pass on the family lineage through the porcupine female, a creature covered with needlelike sharpened quills who is receptive for a few hours a year.

Only we human beings, working with a nearly nonexistent connection to our own instincts, seem to grow increasingly more clueless about basic behavior as we evolve. By the time every religion and governmental body going back to the beginning of civilized life on planet Earth got finished adding its own personally designed improvements to the instruction manual, the rules regarding human mating had become as self-contradicting and confusing as a Japanese game show.

For a look at how things used to work in the simpler but not particularly good old days, witness the past and present women of Kyrgyzstan. Here is a community of lucky gals who, according to *The New York Times,* continue to meet their mates when they are abducted off the street by roving bands of vowel-deprived bachelors. These husbands-to-be rape the women they'd like to spend their lives with in order to make them socially undesirable, knowing this will put them in just the right mood to get married. Once they have been turned into social pariahs, the ladies are left with a choice: be shunned by everyone for the rest of their lives or agree to wedded bliss with their kidnapper-rapist. Out of this romantic Sophie's choice was born a wise old oft-repeated Kyrgyz love homily: "Every good marriage begins in tears."

When I first learned about Kyrgyz courtship, I was horrified and shocked. Then I began to remember something that was told me by my aunt, a sophisticated upper-middle-class housewife from a country known as Long Island. My aunt was a seventysomething, retired, fashionably dressed former docent who never missed a museum opening. One day, while I was suffering from the kind of whiplash that only the sudden collapse of a long-term relationship can inflict, we met for lunch in a trendy Manhattan café. In awe of the contrast between her life history and my own, I asked her to explain the secret of what she constantly referred to as her "happy forty-year marriage." I was expecting to hear a predictable string of platitudes along the lines of "Never go to bed angry" or "Don't take each other for granted."

Instead I got this: "Well, dear, not a day goes by that he doesn't make me cry."

After a rather long silence, I asked, "If he makes you cry every day, why do you call it a happy marriage?"

"Honey," she said, "you learn to take the good with the bad."

That shoulder-shrugging grain-of-salt approach to companionship pretty much summed up the old-school prerequisites for a functional romantic union between two humans. The male half of a lucky couple only needed to earn a living. The female was supposed to have babies, do the housework and the shopping, and get her hair done now and then. And having accomplished that, they were both expected to call whatever else happened as the years went rolling by "a happy marriage."

Not anymore.

Today's peppy modern spouses don't have the patience for a "happy" marriage to someone who makes them cry every day (unless one of them has their own reality show with a thirteen-week guarantee). These days, unhappily married men and women carry within their souls an alternative vision of themselves as a spouse-seeking Ulysses, riding the bounding main on a forty- or fifty-year voyage in search of the perfect soul mate. For those who embark on such a quest, the journey starts out smooth, with the wind in their sails, as they brave the mighty oceans in record time. But by their forties, even the most energetic and gregarious among them are so seasick from the vagaries of dating that they can't face the awful truth: that those first three chemically charged sunlit months of any new relationship are a honeymoon period and a totally false read. During this rosy-hued but unreliable time, plenty of clearly observable bad behavioral patterns go overlooked. It's only in the aftermath of the inevitable wreck that the survivor discovers that buried within the splinters of yet another crashed relationship lies a black box full of recordings picked up by an early tracking system they were choosing to ignore.

Until our culture heeds my pleas for the establishment of a national network of diagnostic stations where one can drop off new love interests and have them evaluated, as one does when purchasing a used car, we will continue to be forced to rely on our instincts. And since no one seems to have the faintest idea what those are, here is a list of specific behavioral clues I have been collecting for the express purpose of helping confused and clueless friends of mine avoid repeating the mistakes I am pretending that I will never make again.

1. AN OBVIOUS LACK OF INTEREST IN YOU

There are so many socially acceptable ways for someone to exhibit a pathological lack of empathy nowadays that this is a very easy symptom to misread. I am here to tell you that if someone is texting, Twittering, and/or checking Facebook while you are talking to them—or using any other app or Internet-related site or device that has been invented since this piece was written—they are telling you as clearly as they can that they are an asshole.

You have the right to command the full attention of the people who are sharing your immediate physical space on any social occasion. And you have the right to expect the attention they give you to be free from lengthy contact with acquaintances at other locations. This kind of behavior is analogous to channel surfing in the middle of a heart-to-heart talk or screaming out someone else's name in bed. Common human decency also dictates that the time you spend together should be free from jiggling legs, drumming fingertips, jangling keys, exasperated sighing, ill-tempered eye rolling, a peevish tone of voice, or any other indications of impatience or boredom. The right to reach over and throttle the perpetrator is one of the few important things our founding fathers forgot to include in the Bill of Rights (along with the right to make a citizen's arrest of a person who replies to something you have said with a famous line from a blockbuster movie).

If you have already observed the behavior above, it would

be unusual if you did not also notice that when you finally do get around to talking, your new companion does not ask you a single question. Do not shrug and think, "No big deal. They're interesting and attractive. We'll get to me soon enough."

Here's what you are not understanding: people who behave like this are generally under the impression that when they are talking about themselves for hours on end, a mutually fascinating conversation *is* taking place.

A friend of mine dated a man who, on the very first date—a time when unnerving truths are often accidentally confessed—mentioned that people often complained that he talked too much. Because she found him interesting, she laughed off his remark as self-deprecating. Then, in the course of things, she found that she could never get a word in edgewise. When she attempted to correct this disparity by charging ahead and trying to insert a few remarks of her own into his monologue, he broke up with her on the grounds that she was making him uncomfortable. And therein lies the detail that she didn't understand: *People like this are only comfortable when they are allowed to be assholes.*

2. A WORRISOME LEVEL OF INTEREST IN YOU

You might think that this is what you have always wanted. At last! A captive audience who can't get enough of you. But it is wise to exercise caution around a person who has a million questions for you yet seems to give out little personal information of their own. More than likely they are keeping something secret—probably something that would change your mind about them if you knew it. They are treading water by distracting you with your own details. Sorry to have to be the one to point this out. I know it was fun to finally hear yourself talk.

3. A WEIRDLY COMPETITIVE ANGLE ON EVERYTHING

As soon as you get a foothold in the conversation, your new companion busts in and says, "Exactly. I know, I know." And the next thing you know, they have hijacked the story to something they thought about while they were forced to endure the inconvenience of having to pretend to be listening to you.

This is sometimes seen walking hand in hand with a tactic I call "topping," wherein someone needs, for some reason, to best your story wherever they can. If you don't feel well, recently they felt much worse than that. If you got a new car, they got one that is so unbelievable it makes your car look substandard.

A third variation on this theme involves someone complaining about their achievements as though they were problems.

> *Example 1:* "I'm so depressed. This huge new book deal I got is putting me into a really bad tax bracket."
> *Example 2:* "My life is such a mess. There are three different incredible guys in love with me right now, but none of them is 'the one.'"

This allows the asshole in question to wear the camouflage of a humble victim, thereby provoking your sympathy rather than your envy. Yet in that very same smooth moment, all the attention is refocused on them and their superior situation! I call this "The Asshole's Double Play."

4. NO IDEA WHO THEY ARE TALKING TO

If someone tells you the same story over and over and doesn't precede the retelling with "Did I tell you this already?," that means (a) they are telling this story to so many people that they cannot keep track of who has heard it before and (b) you are not important enough for them to remember what they have said to you. They live their lives like they are on a personal promotional junket and therefore say the same things to everyone they see. Your job is to offer a round of applause, a few positive affirmations, and a greenroom with a buffet and an open bar. Of course, the latter can, and frequently does, lead to several other very compatible substance abuse problems. Fun!

5. AN INABILITY TO EXPLAIN WHERE THEY HAVE BEEN

Once upon a time I had the experience of dating someone who kept "disappearing." One minute it seemed like we were intimate; the next he was nowhere to be found. In a postcoital afterglow, I'd try to make contact via calls or even presents. When I got no response at all, I would talk to friends about it. Every last one of them seemed to have a lot of insight.

"I think he gets really depressed," said one, who claimed to know him well.

"He's really insecure," said another one.

"He's so freaked out about his career," said a third.

"He was so upset by his divorce that he's still afraid to get too close to someone he loves," said a fourth.

All of these things seemed plausible and made me feel great empathy. How sad for this poor talented guy who tragically undervalued himself and was riddled with pain, uncertainty, and crippling self-doubt. Love had let him down, yes. That was sad. But once he realized that he was "safe" at last, everything would change. What a bright and happy day that would be for us both!

Here's what I forgot: it's not possible to disappear and still be alive. At least not in the dimension in which most of us are still living. I am excluding participants in a witness protection program or international spy ring, because, though not impossible, neither is all that likely. At least among my friends, if they can be believed.

This didn't exactly dawn on me out of the blue. It took an incident in which I learned the names of the tens of other people this particular guy was seeing. And thus did I discover the true meaning of "disappearing" in the context of a romantic entanglement: other cast members in this drama, many with whom you are not yet acquainted but will be. A few may be principal cast. Others may be five-lines-and-under. Possibly they have not heard your name yet, either. Or maybe they have. But best of all, the whole bunch of you are destined to meet under the very worst of circumstances. Go ahead and start figuring out the funny things you are going to say to them all right now.

6. NO WAY TO KEEP THEM FROM GETTING UPSET

Beware the demented fight that erupts out of nowhere. One minute you are talking about potato salad, the next you are being called a castrating bitch. I was once watching TV with a guy who began to exhibit this syndrome right after I mentioned liking an actress on the show that was playing. Next thing I knew, I was being told to leave because the person to whom I was talking had turned my praise for an actress neither of us knew personally into an attack on his character and his place in the world.

When this happens, don't waste your time pacing in a circle with your friends, ruminating about the heartrending details of his unfortunate childhood. It really doesn't matter how much pressure he is under because there is a recession. That's beside the point. You have bumped into an early warning sign of a complicated personality disorder that means no difference of opinion will be tolerated. And yes, unfortunately, this still applies if the person is "really cute."

7. NO WAY TO AVOID THE MANY THINGS THAT THEY FIND ICKY

Be wary of people with juvenile issues about ickiness.

Food is an area of special alarm. (An exception can be made if the person in question is under ten, in which case the problem doesn't fit this essay.) If you notice your new adult companion moving the food around on their plate so it doesn't touch any other food, or picking at something you cooked, then holding it on their fork, sniffing it, and wrinkling their nose like a bunny, watch carefully for other things on this list.

Fussiness about food is one of those traits that come with a list of auxiliary characteristics, including, some will argue, being bad in bed. In fact, since there's no one else here, I will be the one who will argue that. Face it: there are lots of gooey, drippy, damp and clammy, bumpy, and aromatic things that happen in the course of intimate relations with another human being. Even paying special attention to cleanliness and hygiene doesn't change the truth that we are all covered with germs and hairs and assorted viscous fluids that the body itself proudly invented! And there is nothing at all that can be done about the existence of most of these things, short of setting up daily life in a quarantined area or a steaming-hot shower stall.

The same is true for fears about going out, fears about staying in, fears about checking locks or stoves or lights, fears about conspiracies, being watched, or catching an illness. All portend the opposite of a lusty good time. Unless you stand to inherit a lot of money by spending one night in a haunted house with a group of strangers, there's not much to be gained by living in terror.

8. AN ABUNDANCE (OR LACK) OF VANITY

If your new companion shows up smelling bad, it probably isn't because they were so excited about being with you that they forgot to shower. More than likely, they're not tuned in to worrying about other how people see them. In case it's not clear, you *do* want someone who tries to make a good first impression on you. A total lack of awareness about how they are being received means that the person lives in their own parallel, self-absorbed world. If this sounds like something you would find desirable in a companion, I suggest rescuing a dog or a cat.

The opposite condition is equally lethal. A little vanity is fetching: a sign of a healthy ego. But people who are so wrapped up in their looks and the impression they think they are making on others that they cannot kiss you for fear of disturbing the magnificent tableau they have created have relegated you to the role of audience member. If you catch someone checking their reflection in the silverware or sucking in their cheeks and fixing their hair in the shiny surface of their iPhone while you're talking or, worst of all, recording videos of themselves while they're doing any of the above in order to post them on YouTube or Facebook, well, I think by now you know what you must do.

9. TOO MUCH TOO SOON

Exercise extreme caution in the face of any declaration of love that happens too soon. The offer of a commitment from someone who barely knows you is not romantic. It is more likely a sign of lethal flakiness, a smokescreen to distract you from some standard-issue things that you will soon notice are missing, like intimacy, friendship, your Social Security number, your American Express card, your jewelry, your iPod, your keys.

10. TOO GLIB

We're raised to admire people who are charming and witty. Playful banter is the way movie and television couples talk. But remember, in real life there is no TiVo, and a life too full of witty sitcom banter is one of Dante's original nine circles of hell. Think of it: there you are, stuck with someone who is coming up with zany ripostes when you're trying to communicate. Do you really want a smart little answer to everything? When you say, "How are you?," do you really want to hear someone reply, "Compared to what?"

Uh-oh . . . I may have just described myself.

11. AN EERIE RESEMBLANCE TO ONE OR BOTH OF YOUR PARENTS

This is the most important point of all: Beware of anyone who reminds you of the parent with whom you do not get along. Ask yourself this question every time you are instantly attracted to someone problematic: Does this conflict remind me of the ones I had with Mommy or Daddy? If the answer is yes, you have stumbled into Mother Nature's greatest camouflage trick. Shrinks call it repetition compulsion. The mind-bogglingly unfair rules of it are as follows: A brand-new version of the same old parental issues with which you have struggled for years are repackaged and sold back to you in the form of an attractive and compelling member of whichever sex attracts you. To make sure you don't catch on, this new, improved version of Mommy or Daddy is age-appropriate, stylistically perfect for your generation, and available in lavish contemporary colors. But make no mistake: it will turn out that your unconscious picked this fetching but hot-tempered bass player in an indie band, who makes you feel like a misbehaving teenager not because they were perfect but because your unconscious recognizes this sexy new person as a stand-in for your mother.

"But," I can hear you saying, "since I adore my parents, doesn't that mean this relationship I am unconsciously repeating is a good thing?"

Well, maybe. But in that case, you wouldn't be charging into your golden years and still dating assholes, now, would you?

These issues are so complex and confusing that it's fair to wonder if we should all throw up our hands in despair. And I think we all would if it weren't for the unfortunate truth that humans are pack animals. We are meant to live in tribes. Most of us find a life of complete isolation tiring and unnerving. We like the laughter, insights, and distractions that come from being with other people. We also like the sex, the rides to the doctor's office, and the help carrying groceries in from the car.

Therefore, it behooves us to pick our partners as carefully as we can. The only other option is to become the asshole ourselves and try to beat everyone else at their own game. That might explain why, as people get older, they also seem to get meaner and grouchier. They look back on a life of being nice to everyone and think, "Well, that didn't really work, did it? Enough of everyone else's bullshit. This time around, the rest of you assholes can just cope with *me.*"

A Chance to Dance

IT'S FIVE A.M. AND ANDY IS STANDING IN THE DOORWAY OF THE bedroom in which I am fast asleep. Why is he calling my name at this hour? "Merrill!" he says, and then he says it again, louder: "Merrill! Wake up! I think there's a fire."

"Shit," I say, wishing I hadn't just heard that. As I open my eyes, I can hear the sixty-mile-an-hour Santa Ana winds blowing outside.

When I first moved to Southern California at the tail end of the seventies, I loved the Santa Anas. There was something mysterious and sexy about these unseasonably warm winds from the desert that brought an incongruous blast of hot air into the middle of the chillier fall or winter weather. In my mind, their arrival always triggered a chorus of "Here come those Santa Ana winds again" from "Babylon Sisters," a Steely Dan song I love.

It didn't take too many years of living here, however, before the sexiness and mystery morphed into anxiety and dread.

Now the Santa Anas mean only one thing: the crazy people of Southern California have declared another statewide holiday on which they will crawl out of their catacombs and head to one of L.A.'s many dry, overgrown hillsides to dance gaily and fling lit matches. If there is a full moon, like there was last night, well, talk about an embarrassment of riches.

"I think there's a fire," Andy says again.

"Why?" I ask, trying to will it gone. "I didn't hear anything about a fire." When I get up and go to the window, it looks like the Babylon Sisters know whereof they sing. The Santa Anas are flattening all the trees in the front yard down to a forty-five-degree angle, and the early morning sky is coming up a sickly gray-orange, like a Creamsicle that fell into the mud. There are a lot of jarring color combinations in Southern California. You see them every day in someone's fuchsia-and-bright-orange hair or in the chemical concoctions that join forces to create the gorgeous pastel-yellow-khaki-and-magenta smog sunsets. But the scariest colors of them all are hazy yellow, porno pink, salmon, and gray puddling together in the sky, because that means fire. The only thing worse is if you add a sprinkling of ashes, a filthy snow flurry made up of bits and pieces of people's incinerated lives... like we've got today.

Last year, the city I live in caught fire three times. But despite the substantial loss of property, we don't get much sympathy from the rest of Southern California, because we're in the famously un-disadvantaged city of Malibu, fabled in story and song, beloved by movie starlets and other natural disasters. When bad things befall us, everyone seems to feel like we had it coming.

The fire that took place around Thanksgiving 2007 was

a particular standout for a couple of reasons. For one, it was the first fire in which the newscasters seemed to have held a secret meeting and agreed to use the word "event" as often as humanly possible. Suddenly, the Santa Ana winds were a "wind event" and a "Santa Ana event." The fire was, of course, a "fire event." I don't know what committee decided that the words "fire" and "wind" weren't descriptive enough on their own and now needed the word "event" to give them more heft, but every time someone repeated that word, it made me wonder what I'd been charged for my tickets and where I needed to go to apply for a refund.

Standing at the window, looking at the sickly sky, I felt like I was in an encore performance of what was becoming an annual situation: wildfire season and its attendant adversities. In 1993, the first time a uniformed fireman came to my door to announce mandatory evacuation, I had already spent the entire night awake, watching aerial shots of iridescent hot spots in the dry grass while listening to the ravings of over-caffeinated, bedraggled reporters proving their mettle by standing on hillsides looking a little too proud of their charcoal-smudged faces and flapping ponchos as they analyzed every glowing ember like it was a plot point in a horror movie. Because I lived alone at the time, it never felt safe to go to sleep for even a second. I sat there exhausted and wired, hour after hour, watching the path of the advancing fire like it was an approaching enemy army or a news update about a maniac escaped from an asylum who was now running wild in my neighborhood. The broadcasts could show me his mug shot, tell me where he had been and who he had already hurt, but not where he was going to show up next.

About eleven o'clock the following morning, there came

a knock at my door along with the unexpected sight of a uniformed fireman. "We are suggesting that everyone in your
area evacuate at this time," he said. So I put my four large
dogs into my Honda Accord, surrounded by piles of cherished items I had hastily gathered, and drove north on Pacific
Coast Highway to nowhere in particular, my fear but a foot-
note to the ecstasy the dogs were experiencing over the opportunity to ride in the car.

"No, no," I remember saying as they leapt and bounced
with glee, "it's not a walk. It's an *evacuation*."

"Always so negative! Leave it to you to see the downside
of everything," they yelled back in cheery unison. "Stop nit-
picking! We're going for a ride!"

Only later did I learn that I had been the only resident of
my block who had followed instructions and vacated, probably because I was the only woman who lived by herself.
Every male head of every household elected to stay behind
and pursue the long-cherished dream of protecting the
homestead by standing on the roof with a garden hose. No
clearer illustration can be found of the way that men have a
very different relationship to fire than women, to say nothing
of a very different relationship to hoses.

Now here I was again, in a rerun of a situation I had
come to dread. But this time, because there was a man in residence at my house, when the firemen again appeared, I did
not leave.

Unbeknownst to me, I had now joined the ranks of the
"planning to stand on the roof with a hose" faction of my
neighborhood. Our plan, if you could possibly call it that,
was to postpone an evacuation while we kept the fire at bay
by dampening our wood-intensive structures. But because

that meant there was a chance that we would have to evacuate if the hosing plan proved futile, we still had to perform
that most unnerving of all fire-in-the-neighborhood rituals:
deciding which cherished possessions were coming with us if
we did have to leave.

The dogs, the deed to the house, the insurance policies,
the checkbooks, the computers, and the hard drives: these
were no-brainers. Paranoia had caused me to have most of
my important paperwork still in a container I had never un-
packed from a fire threat the previous year.

"I'll be out in the studio," Andy said, as he headed out to
the converted garage to sort through the densest stockpile of
his own personal belongings, some of which were enormous
electronic keyboards.

I stood alone in my office, looking at all my stuff, confronting once again the eccentric collection of souvenirs
from a million particular moments during my twenty-five
years of living here. Obviously, furniture was a moot point.
But in every room of the house a showdown was brewing
among hundreds of inanimate objects, all crying out, "You're
not seriously thinking of leaving me behind, are you?"
Which of these things could I fit into the remaining car space
after my four large dogs had already boarded? Only a handful
of the millions of God-knows-whats were going to make the
trip.

One of my flaws (which I prefer to think of as one of my
endearing traits) is my inability to stop saving worthless
things that I find funny. Take, for example (though I doubt
you will actually want to), an old Xeroxed sign I tore off a
telephone pole because it said, "Turn your canker sores into
cash." So hilarious was it to me at the time that I now have it

preserved in a frame. And it does not want for like-minded company. Every level as well as every vertical surface of my home is littered with something I've saved: ceramic figurines that caught my eye because of their peculiar subject matter, weird foreign food packaging I felt I had to buy because of amusing misspellings. Thus two little overall-clad Amish children holding eggs that are larger than their heads coexist happily alongside my many prized Remnants of Failed Advertising Campaigns. I may have the last two packages of Kraft macaroni and cheese featuring "Andy from Minnesota," a sallow pie-faced teenage boy sporting a Moe Howard haircut who is posed with a big forkful of mac and cheese, his eager mouth agape as he calls out to other teens to "Become a Blue Box Kid!" A week after I bought the packages, they were pulled from the shelves, giving me the responsibility of preserving this piece of poorly conceived macaroni history. Or my mint-condition box of Urkel-Os cereal, which I was prescient enough to buy when it first appeared for sale. Or my spray bottle of Chuck Norris's "KICK brand shoe and boot deodorizer," originally purchased from a coupon in the back of a magazine simply because I was stunned to learn that Chuck Norris was now a player in the world of foot deodorant. Then there were those packages of off-brand freeze-dried squid from a Korean market that are called "Happy Family." Or my cans of "spotted dick," a still-for-sale pudding from England.

But I'm not insane. I knew I couldn't fill up valuable space in my car with spotted dick. So I heaved a remorseful sigh and made a beeline for the twenty-three bulging photo albums in my closet. Damn! If only I had scanned those dinosaurs onto CDs. Okay, . . . which of these photos did I need to see again? The ones from art school and childhood? Yes, of course. Those photos were the only evidence that these things had actually happened. But the trip to Bermuda with an old boyfriend to whom I no longer spoke? Or those pretty shots of the Venice canals and Florence, of which I was once so proud? I could probably find shots just like them, only better, somewhere online now. From golden precious memory to fire fuel in one easy step.

As I moved from room to room, I recalled performing this same unpleasant task during the evacuation of 1993. Back then I'd decided that I would sacrifice all the albums full of the nineties, since presumably there was more ahead. This time the present seemed more pleasant than the past. A new relationship meant a new unfolding narrative. That made sense right now, but would it after everything had been reduced to cinders? What about saving letters from old boyfriends to use as comedy material? Was any of this crap worth money now just because it was old?

No, no, no, I had to argue, grabbing myself by some imaginary lapels that were not on the T-shirt I was wearing. *Do NOT pursue that line of thinking. The only place that road can lead is to your own segment on* Hoarders.

I quickly changed my focus to the three big plastic tubs full of my diaries in the guest room closet: occasional writings that I'd been updating since I was about eight. Did I really want to relive details like "My hair was really oily today"? Or "Lyn's party was horrible. I borrowed a muumuu from Kathy because I thought everyone would be wearing them but only three people did"? Or "Oh God, please please let Jeff call me and I will promise to become a devout Buddhist"?

Absolutely not, I thought, turning my back on them but not really finding it possible to walk away without first packing the little pink-and-red vinyl diaries with the fake locks from elementary school because...well...come on! Aww! My little eight-year-old self, sunburned and overweight, hair pulled back in a too tight ponytail the way my mother insisted, writing embarrassing things I never in a million years could have imagined my much older self would one day not only find funny but reexperience, with almost as much intense embarrassment as I'd felt when I originally wrote them.

I rifled through the messy closet in the guest bedroom, in which I had stashed junior high school drawings of horses, membership cards for stupid fan clubs, and scrapbooks full of photos of cute boys I loved who were on the TV shows I watched. There were also annotated programs from the Beatles concerts I attended and an old pink plastic box that I bought with my allowance when I was ten, embossed with a drawing of a teenage girl wearing a ponytail and talking on the phone alongside the words "My Treasures!" I knew it was stupid and cheesy-looking even back in grade school. But what kind of cold, unfeeling monster would let a "My Treasures!" box melt into a pink puddle?

Next I hit the bathroom. Moisturizer? Definitely. I'd need that. And one lipstick. No, two...er...five. Definitely mascara. And under-eye concealer. Got to have my bite guard, my hot rollers, and just this one other lipstick. And this tube of cortisone cream. And this bottle of Wellbutrin. And my toothbrush, and that's all. Oh my God! Clothes! Better go pack some clothes! But what clothes, exactly? Where was I going? To some motel with a small, kidney-shaped pool that looked out onto a freeway in a nearby city that I had intentionally avoided visiting for years. There I would sit on a musty-smelling bed scrutinizing aerial footage of televised fire devastation for signs of what was happening to my neighborhood. Not really a dress-for-success or formal-evening-wear kind of occasion. Unless all the cheap rooms were booked and I wound up in some overpriced but more glamorous hotel, where the other guests would shun me if I didn't have something nice to wear in the dining room. That meant I had to bring along good clothes? How long was I going to have to stay?

During the course of this rambling internal debate, in which I simultaneously undervalued and overvalued everything in my possession, I realized I'd been pulling clothes off hangers in a frenzy of dissociated energy and throwing them into a suitcase. It was like I was driving drunk. Somehow the suitcase was full but I had no memory of filling it.

Next I made several trips to the car, each with my arms full of scrapbooks, diaries, and paperwork, cramming them in wherever I could, trying to make them fit. My car was now an overstuffed duffel bag, albeit one with an internal combustion engine.

That accomplished, I joined a small group of my neighbors who were standing around in the middle of the street in front of my house: a place where under ordinary circumstances no one would ever be standing. There we gathered like villagers, waiting nervously for some armed invading horde. Every few minutes all conversation would be interrupted by a loud clatter as a helicopter flew overhead on its way toward the ocean to fill up its tanks with water to dump on the fire.

The TV was reporting that there were still sixty-mile-an-hour winds, yet the air on our street was completely still.

This gave us all the impression that we were not in immediate danger, even though we could see a glowing line of embers on distant hilltops. That meant the fire was probably three or four miles away. The TV said it was headed in our direction.

At about noon, the people next door decided that there was no reason not to cook a big breakfast. When they invited us to join them, we were delighted. And so it came to pass that we ate biscuits and gravy in front of a big flat-screen television, staring at vivid real-time footage of the "fire event," which, they now reported, was only two miles away.

While we ate, we debated how we would know when it was the right moment to get in our cars and leave. Predictably, the women were ready to flee. And the men? They were in favor of standing on the roof with their hoses.

"I'm gonna stay," said my neighbor Jack, a big bear of a man. As he spoke, his wife and daughter were packing the car.

"Then I'm staying, too," said Andy.

"But, guys, logically speaking," I said, "if the fire hits our street, how much good are you two going to do standing on the roof with a hose?"

"Come on, Merrill, we're guys, we don't have much left," said Jack. "Don't take everything away from us. Let us have this much."

For the rest of the meal, we channel surfed every local newscast for clues that would help us break the stalemate. With nothing definite to go on, it wasn't long until we wound up back outside, next to our packed cars, staring at the glowing hillside. It was hard to tell if the fire looked worse or better.

That was when someone noticed a uniformed fire official walking into the house across the street. Why was he going in there? Was that a good sign or a bad one? "He's a friend of ours," said the teenage son of the family who lived there. "He will definitely tell us when we have to get out."

This caused us all to begin staring at our neighbors' front door like a bunch of dogs waiting for someone to throw us a ball. About a half hour later, when the same teenage boy emerged from his house and offered a buoyant thumbs-up, we were all both relieved and encouraged.

"We're safe for now," we all said to one another, inexplicably hinging our life-and-death decisions on the hand gestures of a nineteen-year-old occasional lifeguard who I mainly knew as the kid who filled up my recycling bin with empty beer bottles he was hiding from his parents after a big party.

Two extremely long and hazy days later, the fire was extinguished. Ash no longer rained. The sky was once again blue. The streets around my house had been spared. We had been lucky. Not far away, sixty houses had burned to the ground.

Even after the threat had passed, my personal state of emergency continued. I was agitated for another month. Only then did I relax enough to finally unpack my car/suitcase/chest of drawers.

And as I did, I began to examine for the first time the assortment of things I had selected to take with me on my frenetic escape to my brand-new life.

I had plenty of cosmetics—kind of ridiculous, really, since I hear they sell these items in stores. But the contents of my suitcase of clothes was something to behold: five button-down shirts and three pairs of sweatpants, period. I had forgotten to pack any coats, sweaters, underwear, bras, socks, nightgowns, dresses, skirts, or shoes. I'd never looked in my jewelry drawer. I'd taken no paintings off the walls, not even the ones I'd worked on for months; no books, CDs, movies, or high school yearbooks, nothing from my house that, in an ordinary frame of mind, I would have argued passionately against ever throwing away.

If all this stuff on every surface and wall of my home didn't mean enough to try to save in an emergency, why was it cluttering up my life? What were all those clothes in my closet doing there if I didn't like them well enough to bother rescuing them from a fire? And what does it mean that I saved only diaries and photo albums, physical evidence meant to trigger old memories that exist only in my head?

Looking back, the ignored clothes are easy to explain. I was pissed off at them and probably punishing them, for the way they continually disappoint me. When I buy them, it is usually because I think that they will turn me into some new, improved version of myself. Then I catch a glimpse in a mirror, and for some reason, I still don't look much like that six-foot-tall thirteen-year-old model from the Urban Outfitters catalogue, even though we both have bangs. The truth is, I would have loved to throw them all into a big roaring fire, but my practical nature would never allow it. The threat of a dangerous, uncontrollable natural disaster doing the deed for me was a chance to start all over again.

Same with my knickknacks: things that make me laugh are part of what makes life worth living for me. I love my Pez containers, ceramic dogs from thrift stores, and snow globes from airports. But daily life tempts me with an endless array of equally amusing items. Until I move into the dedicated museum space I so richly deserve, I have just so much shelf space to offer my collections. If I lost every single one of these things, I have no doubt at all that my shelves would again be full in a couple of weeks.

On the other hand, there's no starting over with ancient memories. Even though I don't like that many of mine, I feel a certain commitment to preserving all those experiences I carry around in my head, good or bad. The ongoing conversation I can have with the person I was at ten or twelve feels like an odd piece of time travel.

Since I had bothered to save that pink "My Treasures!" box I bought as a kid, I sat down to open it for the first time in decades. Maybe the poor chubby goofball that spent her allowance paying for this thing had left some kind of a message for me inside. I was curious to see what she had to say to her future self, a creature she had never imagined would really exist. I don't remember her having any long-range plans, except for buying a horse. On that count, I had let her down. Would she be mad at me four decades later?

I opened the lid of the box. The clasp was rusty. It had come with a key that I had stopped keeping track of that first week, after I'd learned that the lock could be easily picked with a paper clip.

At the very top was a neatly folded fancy, fluted, twenty-four-inch white ribbon I'd won in a seventh-grade horse show. I'd been proud of it then, though now I wondered if they'd given one to everyone who entered. Underneath the ribbon was a coffee-stained program for a sixth-grade dance recital entitled "A Chance to Dance." At first, I wasn't sure which dance recital this had been. I'd taken a couple of different dance classes when I was a kid. I opened up the cover, and between pages 2 and 3, I found a discolored piece of notebook paper. On it were handwritten instructions along with stick-figure illustrations that showed exactly how to perform the dance I had done that night. Apparently, it had been written for some very unlikely moment in the future when I had forgotten how to re-create this timeless magic.

It began, "Stretch, stretch stretch; Down, up, stand, stretch, stretch stretch, down, up, clap, clap clap." And it ended, "Back to place, jazz arms position, and jazz walk to the back line." All these years later, the moves I described were the one part of the dance I could visualize. I could see the big school auditorium where the dance had taken place on a real stage. There were probably fifteen of us, all in tights without feet, divided into two rows. I was in the back. Was it because I was tall? Or was it because I was clumsy?

Slowly I began to remember how to do the jazz walk, with its accompanying head bobbing and finger snapping. I remembered that when we learned it, a couple of my friends instantly did it more gracefully than I could. I practiced and practiced, in my room in front of the mirror, to no avail; my friends still looked better doing it than I did. By age fourteen I would become so self-conscious that I would call a moratorium on all dancing, forevermore.

Meanwhile, back in the future present: had I been the victim of a devastating fire that had dismantled everything I'd built in my life, there I would have been, sitting on the floor of my new unfurnished rented apartment, trying to comprehend my loss. Well moisturized, and dressed in sweatpants and a button-down shirt, I would have opened up my "My

Treasures!" box, examined my horseback-riding ribbon, and then realized there was nothing left to do but stretch, stretch, stretch, down, up, and clap.

Hopefully there is a learning curve to living through these "annual fire and wind events" and their specter of loss and devastation. Maybe next time I will know how to pack more carefully, remembering to at least take socks, bras, underwear, and shoes. But the experience still coalesces for me in a haunting question: Why don't I go through my house and throw away the things I know I will have to leave behind when this happens again?

It's a good question. And one to which I will give some thought, as I turn, clap, and jazz-walk to the back line.

Selfishness 101 (for Dogs)

I GOT UP EARLY, TOOK ONE LOOK AT THE FRONT PAGE OF THE newspaper, and went right back to bed. A short day, but a satisfying one.

The next time I woke up, two hours later, I was so filled with dread and a sense of foreboding that it felt like waking up in the middle of the night, only brighter. Even surrounded on all sides by four large dogs—a relaxation technique lauded the world over for the many health benefits derived from breathing in big lungfuls of pet dander—I was overwhelmed by anxiety. That's the kind of bracing start a perusal of the morning news can offer a person.

Today I was fretting about how the BP oil spill had not just officially become the worst environmental disaster in our country's history, doing untold damage to an exacting and fragile ecosystem via massive quantities of both oil and toxic dispersant, but also had the ability to corrupt the whole food chain and lead to international environmental contamination, social chaos, governmental collapse, and, eventually, an empty-eyed thug with a tattoo that he'd carved into his own forehead busting down my front door and forcing me to turn my house into his special Malibu breeding farm for morons. I was furious at the way yet another bunch of jowly white men in overpriced casual wear had been in too big of a hurry to devise a worst-case-scenario plan before they'd drilled in the only Gulf of Mexico the planet would ever have. I was also so pissed off and terrified of their plans to drill in the future that I felt envious of the pleasure religious people must take in imagining the bunch of them writhing eternally in the torments of hell. Damn! Something was actually making me wish I believed in hell!

I rolled over and pulled the covers over my head, drowning in terrifying images: me, in a faux-leather Mad Max outfit, my arms and face covered with mud, roaming through a landscape of frenzied mutants and rubble, armed with nothing but a grapefruit knife and the remaining two-thirds of that huge container of flashlight batteries I bought at Costco.

I decided I wouldn't get out of bed until I could figure out some concrete way to be helpful. Should I write a piece about human greed and shortsightedness? Just thinking about the cronyism, the lobbyists, the payoffs at the Minerals Management Service, and the aggressive stupidity of that awful animal-murdering Sarah Palin and her Bible-quoting drill-baby-drill buddies made me breathless with rage. But the only fresh angle I could come up with about it all was imagining the adventures I would have in prison after being arrested at one of her rallies for screaming, "Keep your big mouth shut until you know what you are talking about, you sociopathic simpleton!!" That would probably take place just before I was hauled away in handcuffs for swatting at her with a rolled-up copy of the issue of the *US* magazine that had her daughter and Levi Johnston, reunited, posing on the cover.

Here it was, only ten A.M., and I was already beside myself about the way that selfish, ego-driven people throughout history always seemed to drag the idea of God's approval into their motives. How come these people, who believe that God created everything in a week, are never bothered in the slightest by the fact that He, like Steve Jobs with his "revolutionary" iPhone 4, clearly rushed the human being to market too early? Both were products overflowing with design flaws. But in God's case, what excuse could He have had? Who insisted that He put Himself on such a tight schedule? Did He have shareholders to please? Was some underpublicized Mrs. God bugging Him to hurry up, the way she might have if He'd kept putting off something unpleasant, like cleaning out the garage? And that whole episode in the Garden of Eden— one lady's bad fruit selection was a pretty poor excuse for moving ahead with a line of creatures so full of bugs and malware that they ended up poisoning and devouring their one and only habitat. Come on, God: even hyenas don't go around ruining everything for everyone in their neighborhood.

Tired of my own petulant sermonizing, I returned to the task at hand: trying to come up with one concrete thing I could do to help. A charitable contribution wouldn't make much of a difference, not on my salary. Of course, I could go to Louisiana to help clean oil off of pelicans, but unless I committed to moving there, I'd feel like a fickle hobbyist. Or . . . now, this was a long shot, but . . . what if I could just bring some of the oily pelicans back here to live at my house, where I could clean them and tend them and protect them from further harm until they were out of danger and feeling much better? I could probably fit about five hundred birds into my house. They could nest on my chairs and couches! And since I live only a half mile from the ocean, we could take frequent field trips to the beach!

It wouldn't be an easy transition. I would probably have to invent a group pelican leashing system. But I was up to the task.

Only one hitch: the new resident birds might have a problem getting along with my dogs.

But in this case, *too bad for the dogs!* Their lives weren't being threatened, unless you counted their testy relationship with the equally spoiled dogs on the other side of the fence.

No, until the birds were steady and able to get on their feet, I would lock the dogs in the back of the house. Sure, after being catered to their whole lives, they'd be pissed. But in this time of crisis, we the fortunate ones needed to put ourselves second. We'd all have to look at the bigger picture

"Okay, you guys," I said as the four of them gathered around me on the bed, staring at me as a way to pressure me to get up and feed them. "There are four-point-two million gallons of oil a day pouring into the Gulf of Mexico. It's a horrible disaster for more reasons than I think your attention spans will allow me to enumerate. So here's my point: we cannot all sit calmly by and watch as the world is destroyed by selfish, greedy people. We have to help out wherever we can. Are you with me?"

No one said a word.

"I'm going to take that as a yes," I continued, "because

we all need to pitch in for the greater good. I want you to re-member what I just said when a bunch of pelicans from Louisiana show up at the house."

The dogs kept staring at me.

"So, you all understand what I'm proposing?" I asked. "While I am finding out if I need to get a sanctuary permit or what, I want the four of you to readjust how you feel about birds. I know you find them irritating for some reason, but under these circumstances I will expect you to behave. Even though sacrifice is a concept with which you are not too fa-miliar."

Hedda yawned. "We're more familiar than you think. What do you call hanging around watching you for hours on end?"

"I always wondered why we did that," said Ginger.

"She apparently needs an audience," said Puppyboy. "No one knows why."

"That's very insulting," I snapped. "I don't *need* an audi-ence. And if I did, you guys are the last ones I would pick. But even if what you say is true, how is that a sacrifice? I'm far and away the most entertaining thing in your lives."

"You don't think we'd rather be out running in traffic?" Hedda snorted.

"Well, maybe, but you're forgetting: you have it pretty easy around here. Not one of you ever helps out. And you're all middle-aged now, which is much too old to be so selfish."

"And by selfish you mean . . . what exactly?" said Ginger.

"The act of placing one's own needs or desires above the needs or desires of others," I said. "I don't suppose that rings a bell with any of you?"

"Yes! It does with me," said Puppyboy. "I *invented* that!"

"You didn't invent it," said Jimmy. "I was doing that way before I knew who you were."

"No, you're both not understanding," I said. "Selfishness is *not* considered a good thing. I am talking about being oblivious to anyone's feelings but your own. The only thing the four of you care about is yourselves."

"That's some serious bullshit," said Puppyboy. "Every creature in all of nature knows that putting yourself first is pure instinct. If I'm not thinking about myself, I am not running at full capacity. Therefore I am endangering the species and putting the ecosystem at risk. Now, *that* is my definition of something bad."

"I guess the problem is, these instincts of yours work better in the wilderness than in a domestic setting," I said. "Like it or not, we live not by instincts but by human rules. And since this is my house, I get to say which rules apply."

"So you're the selfish one?" said Ginger.

"No, the word 'selfish' doesn't apply in this case, because I go out of my way to make the four of you extremely comfortable," I said.

"You ignore me a lot," said Puppyboy.

"I can show you a perfect example of selfish, thoughtless behavior right this very minute," I went on, ignoring him. "Look at Ginger. She is standing on top of a newspaper I'm reading."

"I'm not doing anything," said Ginger, flinching as though I were going to hit her.

"Yes, you are. And stop flinching. I'm not going to hit you," I said. "All I'm asking is that you take a moment to think about where you're standing before you decide to stand there."

She looked at me with the uncomprehending eyes of a chicken.

"Ginger, listen," I said. "I am very important to your survival. To frame it in terms of this whole BP oil spill scenario, in this household I am the ocean and you are the pelican. If we want to share our environment, we must live in harmony with each other. Therefore, you must constantly ask yourself, 'Am I standing on something that is important to Merrill?' If the answer is yes, then you must stop standing on whatever it happens to be: the front page of my *New York Times,* the manuscript I am writing, my freshly laundered shirt, my head. . . . And that goes triple for my laptop."

"*I* never stand on your newspaper," said Pup.

"True. But you, Puppyboy, are selfish in other ways," I went on. "For instance, the way you think we're all supposed to stop whatever we're doing whenever you show up with a ball."

"What?" said Pup, so angry he was now avoiding my gaze. "That is pure generosity of spirit! I look around and see that you're sitting there, bored out of your skull . . . doing absolutely nothing . . ."

"You mean like when I'm taking a bath?" I countered. "And you are dropping balls into the tub? Or when I'm watching a movie and you are piling balls onto my lap?"

"Exactly," said Puppyboy. "And, I would like to point out, I bring the balls right to you. You don't have to move even an inch. For instance, right now, I see you lying there by your newspapers, intending to go back to sleep. So . . . very quietly . . . I will drop a ball on top of your chest . . . a preemptive strike that will turn your boring, monotonous life into a Technicolor 3-D videogame!"

"You don't seem to comprehend that when I am sleeping, I am not bored," I said. "And when I am reading, I am not bored. Well, sometimes I am. But the important thing here is that for you to insist that I change my whole orientation to the one that interests you makes *you* selfish. Not me."

"Hold on a second," said Pup. "You have it backwards. When you are just sitting in a container of water, doing nothing, *you* are placing your needs ahead of everyone else's. Everyone else probably wants to go for a walk, which is about survival and hunting and marking territory. And there you are, for no good reason lying down in a container of water."

"Wrong," I said, sitting up, finally realizing that going back to sleep was not going to be possible. "Bathing *is* part of survival. And, Ginger, I have asked you twice now to get off of my newspaper. I haven't finished reading all of today's horrible stories."

"I'm still not sure why you aren't grateful that I do this," said Ginger. "Why do you even want to read about things that are horrible?"

"By the way: BREAKFAST!" said Hedda. "I just thought I'd put that out there. For discussion or whatever."

"I read about horrible things, Ginger, because it's part of my responsibility as a member of society to keep abreast of what is going on, no matter how upsetting," I said. "In today's world we are all part of one big ecosystem that connects us to one another. So to honor this I need to know about the confusing and horrifying things that people are doing all over the planet."

"Ah. I see," said Ginger. "And once you know about

these things, are you going to bring them all here to the house to live so you can fix them? Like you want to do with the pelicans?"

"Well, no..." I said. "Usually I just sign an online petition or something."

"What does that do?" asked Ginger.

"Gives a bunch of spammers my email address," I said. "But my only other option is to donate money to a charity where I have no way of knowing if it goes to pay for environmental cleanup or to buy a case of Mountain Dew Code Red for some teenage volunteer."

"Then why bother at all?" said Puppyboy. "Especially when there is a satisfying and rousing game of ball directly in front of you?"

"Because I would feel *selfish* if I didn't," I said. "That's what I'm trying to teach you guys today. We all need to be out there on the front lines, telling the truth about evil. We should be in the Congo and the Sudan protecting the innocent, bringing food to the children of Darfur or aid to the earthquake victims of Haiti, and when we're done with all that, there are oil-soaked pelicans to clean...the very ones who I hope will soon be living with us here at this house."

"Which reminds me: breakfast!" said Hedda. "Just throwing that out there again."

"And also: you can't leave," said Ginger. "Who would be here to open the cans for us?"

"Believe me, I've used your total dependency on me as an excuse for staying home far too often," I admitted, rolling over onto my other side so I could avoid their needy stares. "We're all very selfish. And we live in a selfish, amoral world.

The implications of this stuff are so far-reaching and upsetting that right now I'm going back to sleep for the rest of the day."

I had no sooner pulled the pillow over my head than I heard the loud tearing and crunching sound of Ginger digging a hole in the center of my carefully folded *New York Times*. In seconds she had made herself a comfortable nest of shredded paper.

"For the last time, Ginger: Get off my newspapers. NOW!" I shouted. "Have I been talking to myself? Have any of you even heard a single word I said?"

"Calm down," Hedda snapped at me as Ginger jumped off the bed, kicking a trail of torn index-card-sized pieces of paper into the air behind her. "No reason to get hysterical. Ginger's a little slow."

"Oh, but you're the big genius," said Puppyboy. "Miss Barks-at-Anyone-Who-Comes-in-the-Door-Wearing-a-Hat."

"I just want to make sure that the rest of you understand what *she* is saying," said Hedda, staring at me. "That we all have to work together for the good of the group. A group, as I understand it, of which she is the self-appointed leader. Which also means that *she* needs to get us *some breakfast right now* since the group is in total agreement that everyone needs to eat."

"Fine," I groaned, heaving a big sigh as I came to terms with the fact that my plans for additional sleeping had been hijacked. My newspaper was destroyed. My bed was covered with filthy tennis balls and torn shreds of paper. "I thought I might try to sleep a little longer, but to hell with me." I hoisted myself out of bed and put on a sweater. Then I headed into the kitchen, gathering dog bowls from the floor as I walked, the way a movie theater janitor gathers empty popcorn boxes.

"Obviously, if I want to save the world, I will have to do it alone," I heard myself muttering out loud as I opened the first can of dog food. "The four of you have proven that you are all too self-absorbed. There's nothing I can depend on you to do, ever—"

"Except to hang around you, wherever you happen to be," Ginger interrupted, staring hard at the can of food.

"And always act thrilled to see you," said Jimmy, drooling.

"Whether we feel like it or not," Hedda added, thumping her tail lazily as a way of asking me to hurry up. "Whether you look good or bad. Or have done anything worthwhile."

"Who else would sit waiting, staring, ecstatic whenever you come in the door?" said Puppyboy. "Even when you've done nothing that I can see to deserve it?"

"And despite the fact that the mere sight of you reminds us of food," said Hedda.

"So you're not really even happy to see me," I said, hurt. "It's just an act because you associate me with food?"

"Well, yes," said Ginger. "But there's more to it than that."

"Even in an environmental catastrophe or a financial meltdown, we will still act glad to see you," said Hedda. "This house could be coated in oil and toxic solvent. We will act like you're totally great."

"Name someone, anyone else, who guarantees that kind of service," challenged Jimmy.

"Not occasionally, but twenty-four hours a day," said Hedda.

"Even *after* we have thrown up on every surface we could," said Ginger. "We may have ruined your wood floors and your rugs. We may have pissed on your comforter. Even then, we will seem so happy to see you it will be like it all never happened. Or I will, at least."

"Don't pretend it's just you," Hedda chimed in. "I do the same thing but much better."

"Neither of you is half as good at it as me," Jimmy interrupted.

"That all counts for something, doesn't it?" said Puppy-boy, who was hard to understand because his mouth was entirely filled with a deflated basketball.

"I guess it does," I said, nodding silently to myself as I portioned some food into each of their bowls.

Medusa's Sister

I COULDN'T WAIT TO GRADUATE FROM HIGH SCHOOL AND LEAVE home for the comforts of an institution of higher learning that would let me make art day and night. My parents were fine with the leaving home part but didn't like the idea of being saddled with the crushing tuition payments of an art school. Back then, the University of California was an amazing bargain for state residents, so I was under strict instructions to pick the UC campus to which I wanted to apply.

Since those were the rules, there was one and only one campus for me: Berkeley.

In those days, "Berkeley" was synonymous with "lunacy." There were riots for every occasion. There were rallies for organizations that I never would have thought could have sufficient funding to make the Xerox copies needed to let people know they existed. The entrance to the campus was like a street fair that forgot what holiday it was celebrating. Every day I saw people who wouldn't think twice about wearing a cheese grater or a hot water bottle as an accessory.

My parents were aware of this, and so to make sure there was some counterpoint, they signed me in to the oldest and most traditional of all the women's dorms on campus. It was called Stern Hall and it came complete with a "dorm mother": a square-shaped dowager with a headful of big stiff white hair who, if this had been the 1930s, would have been cast as Mrs. Bissonette, the nettlesome wife of W. C. Fields. Her job was to make sure the "history and legacy" of Stern Hall were carried forth by its current residents. She wasn't the type of person I would have expected to find surviving in the wilds of Berkeley, any more than I would have expected to find a ring-tailed lemur. But there she was, in her knee-length, pastel frock and low-heeled pumps, presiding over the mandatory dorm meetings.

This was so not what I'd had in mind.

I was already pretending that Berkeley was actually an art school, albeit one with a football team and a bunch of other required courses. It was the art classes that fed my sense of identity. Everything about them felt right. From the very first day, I was in love with the poetry and tragedy that being an art student conferred on me. When I skulked around the long, echoing halls of Kroeber Hall, the concrete-and-glass art building, I was transformed from an insecure, identity-crisis-riddled middle-class girl to a dark, potentially brilliant Chekhovian creature: too sensitive and perceptive for your world. Now if I threatened to kill myself, I'd be taking with me a whole catalogue's worth of never-to-be-realized mixed-media masterpieces. Very nice.

It took only a couple of weeks for me to begin to fine-tune the details of my new image so that they lined up properly with those of an Important Artist in Training. Through careful observation and data gathering, I ascertained that the Important Artists of the Bay Area dressed like ranch hands. They drank Jack Daniel's straight up from unwashed water glasses, rolled their own cigarettes, and lived in warehouses where they also worked. Niceties like furniture and expensive clothes were an afterthought for these impressive men, because their art involved dangerous equipment, like acetylene torches, table saws, and Cor-Ten steel. Like everything else that mattered, real art was a man's job. So I began to make sculpture, not because I liked to work in three dimensions but because of the sense of macho competence I got from knowing how to operate power tools. Though I didn't smoke yet, I was working on it, aware that I needed a hand-rolled cig balancing on my lower lip when I put on the goggles and stood in that cyclone of sawdust.

The more I hung around the art department, the more embarrassed I became about the gentility expected from me at Stern Hall. No one could know I lived there or hear that I had to show up at those obligatory dorm meetings. They were more embarrassing than living at home with my parents.

That first dorm meeting got off to a rousing start when Mrs. Bissonette remarked, proudly and without a trace of irony, that this very dorm had risen to the heights throughout the years of Berkeley's star-studded past by having its residents associated with a traditional image of elegance. "The women of Stern Hall spend hours on their hairdos, and it's the pride and glory of the dorm," she said, reflecting a value system so out of touch with Berkeley in the late sixties that for a moment I wondered if we were all performing in a satirical improv group sketch.

Even more galling to me was another of our house rules: the gloriously coiffed women of Stern Hall, Mrs. Bissonette explained, were required to participate in a predinner ritual that was like something out of the antebellum South. At five-thirty we all had to gather at the head of a spiral staircase, in our dinner dresses, and follow Mrs. Bissonette on a magnificent promenade to the dining room, *Gone with the Wind*–style.

I did not take this news well.

First of all, I had brought just one dress to school with me, and that was only after a heated argument with my mother. Every other piece of my current clothing I was carefully allowing to acquire a patina of random paint splatters, the better to reflect the seriousness of my artistic intentions.

When the dorm meeting came to a close, I quickly met two other like-minded girls who were similarly offended by this indignity. The three of us began plotting a campaign of protest. The best we could come up with on short notice was the idea of wearing our so-called dinner dresses on top of whatever jeans ensemble we had worn to class that day.

And the very next evening, we put our plan in motion. When the dinner promenade was lining up, I arrived wearing my navy blue sleeveless A-line sheath over a black-and-purple striped T-shirt, a pair of jeans with one knee ripped open, and paint-splattered cowboy boots.

It took only three days of these forward-thinking fashion statements before my two new best friends and I received word that Mrs. Bissonette wanted to talk with us. We were summoned to the dorm mother suite, where she sat in una-mused silence, seeking an explanation of our behavior.

"It just doesn't seem fair to force me to take time off from making art to change into a dress for dinner, knowing that a few minutes after that I'll have to change right back into work clothes again," I explained.

"Maybe you are not a good fit for Stern Hall," said Mrs. Bissonette.

Those were the ten words I'd been longing to hear.

From there it was a mere hop, skip, and a jump to forging my parents' signatures on a release form, so that we three renegades could rent an apartment off campus. Now there would be nothing keeping us from setting up the kind of free-spirited creative environment befitting individuals of limitless abilities such as ourselves who were ready to take our place as the kind of human beings to whom the next century would no doubt owe a great debt of thanks.

Our new apartment was a four-room promised land in a two-story stucco building, a mere fifteen-minute bike ride from campus. We didn't have furniture. Furniture was but a first unnecessary step toward a stifling life devoid of all meaning. Besides, the place came with a card table and a couple of folding chairs. As far as I was concerned, it was fully furnished.

Everything about this apartment was perfect. Imagine a refrigerator that contained only the food my friends and I put into it! I could be on an unending diet of only celery and sugar-free Jell-O and no one would ever dream of saying a word! At last I had a place I was proud of, where I could invite the right kind of interesting young man in for a cup of weird licorice-smelling tea in a room lit only by scented candles, as I did that very first week, when a guy from my Basic Design class stopped by at midnight. There we were, at the card table, inhaling cinnamon in a flickering open flame, listening to the new Doors album and discussing existence while also playing with a can of rubber cement. We were layering globs of it on the tabletop to form interesting sculptural shapes that were even more awesome when you set parts of them on fire. Okay, yes, for a few minutes we set the whole table on fire. But we put it right out again with a couple of big pots of water. And by the end of the evening, you could hardly see the black smoke stains way up there on the ceiling of the kitchen.

Next thing I knew, spring quarter was over and my roommates were packing their suitcases and heading home for the summer. Though I'd landed a part-time job as a counter girl at the Lunch Box in Berkeley, it didn't pay enough for me to cover the rent for our three-bedroom apartment alone. I couldn't bear the idea of giving up my freedom yet was unable to figure out where to find more roommates on such short notice.

Somehow I managed to convince my parents to let me enroll in summer quarter. I could stay on in Berkeley and live in some much cheaper apartment that I swore I was going to be able to find. The most compelling part of my argument involved a couple of very famous visiting art professors who would be teaching just this one summer, then never again. For a passionate, committed art student such as myself, I pleaded, it was the kind of rare opportunity that couldn't be missed.

It didn't take me long to find that cheaper apartment on the Oakland-Berkeley border: three rooms in a row, railroad-style, with a Murphy bed, on the ground floor of another old stucco building. And no, I still wasn't planning on having furniture. Free of the compromises required by having room-mates, I seized the opportunity to set up my new apartment the way all the big boys did: as a studio. I would transform my little flat into an enormous warehouse full of important art. Immediately I began setting aside a little money from every paycheck at the Lunch Box to buy the things I knew I needed more than tables and chairs: a jigsaw, a belt sander, and a power drill.

The day I walked out of the hardware store as a full-fledged power tool owner was a very proud day for me indeed. I was holding real physical evidence that I had transcended every stereotype and limitation associated with my gender. There could no longer be any doubt that I was an artist of substance, despite the fact that my version of the requisite ranch-hand/artist persona now sometimes included miniskirts with knee-length high-heeled boots.

Summer quarter seemed to be shaping up very nicely. I got in line early enough to be enrolled in all the classes I wanted. Plus, even more validation was waiting around the bend. One of the Internationally Famous Art Professors, a man who'd had solo shows at the Metropolitan Museum of Art and the Marlborough Gallery in New York and London, began to show special interest in me! Not only did I get into his class, but I was the one he invited out for coffee during our midmorning breaks! I could hardly believe my good fortune.

The Internationally Famous Art Professor was a medium-sized bookish-looking guy with short brown hair, horn-rimmed glasses, and a trim graying beard. He wasn't young or hip or especially fun to talk to, like my classmates. But I didn't really expect that from someone so prominent in his field. When you were that successful you didn't really have to say much, I figured. Talk was cheap; fun was overrated anyway. Learning to look past uncomfortable silences and see the depth lurking beneath them was part of the privilege of knowing a real art star.

I never said much during our class breaks together. Just being allowed to stand there and sip my coffee, while my professor and his friends held forth, seemed like reward enough. The extra attention he lavished on me made me feel so special that I began to carry myself in a way that reflected my newfound status. I felt more three-dimensional. I had a sense of place and weight in the world. I began to develop an image of myself as magnetic and powerful, as someone of whom you should be aware.

Still, when Mr. Internationally Famous asked me matter-of-factly, at the end of class one Friday, if I was available to go out with him the following night, I wasn't sure, at first, if I was understanding him correctly. After the words finally sank in, no other answer made sense except yes.

It never occurred to me to think of him as anything but a mentor. It didn't seem possible that he was asking me out on a "date." I wasn't even nineteen. He was, like, forty-five or something: much too old to be attractive, an adjustment I assumed all people over forty were aware of and had learned to deal with somehow.

I remember standing in front of the small closet in the corner of my studio, staring at my unexciting wardrobe, not sure what to wear for this occasion. It didn't seem right to show up in jeans for a Saturday night outing with an internationally renowned art star. I tried on different combinations of the various things I owned, until I finally settled on a short navy blue belted T-shirt dress with white edging and my tan high-heeled boots. The boots, I hoped, added a certain no-nonsense ready-for-action gravitas to the girlyness of wearing a dress.

Standing on the edge of the bathtub so I could see my reflection in the medicine cabinet mirror, I felt bohemian yet fetching, stylish yet gutsy. I was an artist but still a girl.

I took the bus over to the condo complex where Mr. Internationally Famous was living for the summer. There I learned that an amazing piece of synchronicity had occurred. Joining us that evening was the other famous visiting art professor, who, unbelievably, was also mentoring a girl genius from his class! What a coincidence: two future art world heavyweights, both teenage girls, both being mentored by Internationally Famous Art Professors at the same place and time! What were the chances?

As I entered the completely silent room, the second professor and his mentee were on the couch, sipping glasses of white wine. Everyone was gracious and friendly, but it all felt awkward right away. For brilliant men who spent their free time supervising the hanging of their work in world-class museums, neither had anything much to say tonight.

While my professor went off to fetch me a glass of wine, I strolled around the mostly empty room, looking for things to examine. Unfortunately, the shelves of the temporary residence were empty and the walls uncomfortably bare.

The next time I tuned back in to the conversation, the

other art professor was saying something on the topic of the orgies he claimed were everywhere in Berkeley that summer. This came as a big surprise to me. Not only had I never seen hide nor hair of an orgy, I couldn't recall the topic ever being mentioned. But I quickly tamped down my embarrassment by telling myself that anything either of these brilliant guys might say was just more grist for the mill that fed their art. Since I had nothing at all to add, except my stupid discomfort, I feigned interest in the view of the rest of the apartment house from the concrete patio instead.

Soon it was time for us to leave, so we all got in my teacher's VW Bug and drove across the Bay Bridge to San Francisco. Our dinner destination was a Basque family-style restaurant in the North Beach section, just down the block from the Condor and a couple of other very famous topless-dancer bars. The whole neighborhood was lit with three-story neon signs of naked girls with flashing lightbulbs for nipples.

Inside the restaurant, the four of us joined a long table full of other diners. That was fine with me, since I was still having trouble thinking of things to say. I knew nothing about Victorian erotica, another topic that kept surfacing, but then again...I was an interloper, a student, a neophyte. I was there to learn. My opinions were beside the point.

After dinner, the four of us walked up the block to see a show by Charles Pierce, an internationally famous female impersonator. International fame seemed to be everywhere that night. Mr. Pierce was performing in a small club with an ornate, gilded stage that had many rows of folding metal chairs set up in front of it. He opened with his impression of Bette Davis doing Scarlett O'Hara on a swing covered in plastic flowers. The mostly gay male audience began to swoon. This was my first female-impersonation show, though I definitely knew all about them, because I had been living for years in the Bay Area. Drag shows were as key to the local economy as crab fishermen and mime troupes. The idea of a man pretending to be a woman didn't seem that weird to me, though I was also embarrassed to admit that I wasn't sure why the idea of a man in a dress and a wig was supposed to be so awe-inspiring. Then it dawned on me: maybe this was my Toulouse-Lautrec at the Moulin Rouge moment! Seeing it through an art student lens, I realized that I might right now be in the midst of the new avant-garde...the very people who were blazing the trails through the future of art history! Maybe I would find my place among them as one of the very few female artists who knew her way around the demi-monde. All I had to do was keep my mouth shut and pay attention.

That was what I was thinking when the Internationally Famous Art Professor leaned over and put his tongue in my ear. This ear bath continued for so long that it seemed to require some kind of reaction. The only one I could find inside me was coiled like a snake and shaped like the words "Uh-oh."

I knew I was supposed to find this pleasurable. Since I didn't, I tried to turn up the corners of my mouth and arrange my face accordingly. The last thing I wanted to do was offend the Internationally Famous Art Professor.

By the end of the evening, when Mr. IFAP pulled his Volkswagen up to the curb in front of my apartment to drop me off, I was still flummoxed. "Thank you so much," I stammered, my hand on the car door handle as I prepared to let myself out. He stared at me expectantly, waiting for me to speak.

"Would you like to come in for some tea?" I finally asked, not because I wanted to spend more time with him but because I couldn't bring myself to be anything but gracious to Mr. IFAP. Anyway, how bad would it be to have him come in and see my studio?

And what timing! As of today, there was even a place to sit in my apartment: a rotting rattan love seat I had taken from the curb across the street before garbage pickup removed it forever. Now it faced into a room that was full of workbenches, and sawhorses topped by doors so they could also double as worktables. The floor of the room itself was covered with piles of sawdust, proudly unswept: proof that I didn't just own power tools, I also knew how to use them.

"Come sit next to me," he said, patting the seat beside him as I approached carrying tea, served in ceramic cups from my Boy Scout mug collection, each one emblazoned with an individual troop insignia. For Mr. IFAP, my favorite: Region Twelve, decorated with a decal of an angry black-and-red bull's head in a yellow circle.

My short-range plan was to entertain Mr. IFAP with my enormous shoe box full of unintentionally funny postcards, which I had been collecting since high school. Ceremoniously, I removed the box from the cabinet and placed it on the rattan seat between us. Then I began to pull out a few of my favorites, many of which I had sorted by themes. I had at least ten different ones that featured a photo of a giant trout filling the bed of a pickup truck, though some were "strapped" to

the side of an only slightly larger horse. They all said something like "Caught a FAIR-sized trout today."

I was prepared to move from there to a second, equally
amusing theme: postcards featuring lots of different photos of
squirrels eating acorns, all of them captioned "Nutty About
Nuts." After that, I would break out the cards spotlighting
enormous fruits and vegetables. But before I could locate the
three different versions of giant cabbages loaded onto flatbed
train cars, Mr. IFAP leaned in to kiss me.

My worst fears were confirmed.

I was so uninterested in kissing this blocky, bearded old
guy that I had no idea what facial expression to plaster on this
time. Kissing him was like making out with Santa.

In retrospect, I probably looked to him like a girl who
had been around. Maybe my short skirt and my high boots
and my foul mouth had him fooled. Or the way I had acted
blasé when he talked about all the people he knew who
had orgies and liked Victorian erotica. Maybe he assumed I
liked that stuff, too. He almost certainly would have been
surprised to learn that I knew a lot more about power tools
and funny postcards than I did about human sexuality. So far,
I had only slept with the Mechanical Man. And he had been
such a puzzling first encounter that just a day or two before I
had asked a friend, "What does it mean when a guy says, 'Did
you come?' Come where?"

"I'm not sure," she had replied. "I think it has something
to do with having an orgasm."

"Seriously?" I said.

Next thing I knew, the Internationally Famous Art Professor and I were on my Murphy bed having sex because it

seemed rude to say no to him. He was my professor. He was a big famous guy. He was Santa Claus!

When I opened my mouth to form the words that would excuse me from participating, nothing came out.

So Mr. IFAP took his place as the second guy in the sex parade. To be fair, despite his advanced age he was a much better partner than the Mechanical Man. Yet I was still left wondering what it was about the act of intercourse that had captivated the souls of writers and poets for centuries.

The third guy I had sex with broke into my apartment the night after my big date with the Internationally Famous Art Professor.

I was asleep in my Murphy bed, in the farthest of the three rooms that stretched out in a row from the front door, when I awoke to a strange noise. I thought it was the wind rattling a window in the living room. When I stumbled out to fix the problem, only half awake, I saw a guy in a dark jacket standing beside the sawhorses. I froze as I tried to make the image compute, thinking, *What about this don't I understand?*

Before I had an answer, he had moved toward me, grabbed me, and put his hand over my mouth. A wild electrical charge went through my brain, an exploding flashbulb. *Who is he? What is he doing here?*

And then my very next thought, swear to God, was *Jesus Christ. He's here to steal my power tools.*

But I guess the guy must have had his own electric sander and band saw because he appeared to be ignoring my workbench entirely. The feeling of his big warm hand covering my mouth was an awful sensation.

I remember him saying something about having a knife as he dragged me to my bedroom and threw me on the bed. My mind was racing, searching for a strategy, a plan of escape. In the Abnormal Psychology 101 class I was taking, I had learned that rape was not about sex but about power. If sub-duing a struggling woman was a turn-on, then I would pre-tend to pass out. That might buy me some time.

So I went limp.

When he moved one of my arms or legs, I let it fall, like a corpse. When he started pulling off the T-shirt I was sleep-ing in, I let my lower jaw hang open, my tongue fall out until it was resting on my bottom lip. Keeping my eyes closed during all this was the real challenge. My eyelids didn't want to relax. But I guess it all worked, because only a few minutes after it had begun, he got up and left the room.

Had he gone to get the power tools? Had he gone to get some water to throw on me to try to revive me? I didn't wait to find out. His blue nylon windbreaker was still on the edge of the bed when I jumped up, locked the bedroom door, and started to scream.

Then I called 911.

By the time the police arrived, I was in my bedroom alone, sobbing, dressed in the first clothes I could find . . . the ones on the floor by the bed: my short T-shirt dress and a pair of high leather boots. The policemen barely spoke to me as they dusted the walls for fingerprints. I wondered if they thought of me as another stupid, weird Berkeley chick. I wondered if I was one.

Next thing I knew I was boarding an ambulance.

I barely recognized my reflection in the thick glass door

as I was escorted into a county hospital emergency room somewhere in Oakland. With my hair sticking out at odd angles and my makeup smeared, I looked like I'd been trick-or-treating.

Taking a seat by the wall in the waiting area, I settled into staring. I had no attention span for paging through *Redbook*, the only magazine in the room and one I'd never liked under the best of circumstances. That the whole incident had even happened was just beginning to sink in. It was still hard to believe. I felt sad and alone, but there was no one I could think of to call. Most of my friends had gone home to some other state for the summer. I definitely didn't want to involve my parents in this and take on their predictable rage. I could hear my father's "beardo weirdo" rants echoing over the cacophony of my mother's hysteria. So I sat very still and gazed, glassy-eyed, into the middle distance, seeing nothing, occasionally looking over at the young mom directly across the room from me, who was waiting for someone while keeping an eye on her young son.

Probably out of boredom, the little boy was drawn toward me. He was seven or eight and intruding into my personal space in the way that only a guileless grade school kid can. He was clearly eager for any kind of distraction in a room that offered not a single intriguing square inch.

I sat miserable and silent, trying to ignore him.

"Lady," he finally said, positioning himself right in front of me, then cocking his head and squinting. "If you ain't Medusa, you is Medusa's sister."

Stunned that a kid his age had referenced Medusa, I started to laugh.

"You're right." I nodded. "I'm her sister. That's correct."

His mother called him back to her side and he scampered off.

But as I continued to sit there, his remark made me laugh again and again. In my new role as Medusa's sister, I was somehow better equipped to cope and put things in perspective. I'd entered the hospital a sniveling, disheveled victim who had been crushed by a cruel, violent encounter. But I would be leaving an awe-inspiring, terrifying Gorgon: a winged woman with brass hands who could turn a man to stone with her piercing stare. Or, should I say, the *sister* of a woman who could do all of that, but come on! It ran in the family! I had pull with her. She would listen to me. We were on very good terms, me and my sister Medusa.

A short while later, the hospital released me. I don't remember much about the medical exam. When I was standing at the reception desk, checking out, I became aware that I had to call someone for a ride home.

This was a problem. The only person I knew with a car was Mr. IFAP.

"Hi. I'm sorry to bother you," I said, aware of voices and laughter in the room where he had answered the phone. Apparently he was entertaining guests again. "I'm calling from a hospital emergency room. And I...well...someone broke into my apartment and I don't have anyone to give me a ride home now."

Much to my relief, he agreed to come get me, even though he was already in the middle of mentoring another young art genius.

I babbled incomprehensibly as IFAP and his other prodigy drove me back to the scene of the crime, where they dropped me off curbside so they could make a U-turn and head back to their previously scheduled event.

I stood alone in the foyer of my apartment house, afraid to open the door to my apartment. I was not eager to face a long night filled with the loud silence of walls full of dusted black fingerprints. What if my attacker was nearby, watching me? Or worse, what if he was already back inside, waiting for me to return?

It was in this moment that I met my neighbors for the first time.

"Are you okay?" said a slim blond man, peering out from behind the chain on the door of the apartment across from mine. "What happened?"

Looking more closely, I could see that he and his companion were in drag.

"Well, I guess I'm okay," I said. "Except for . . . you probably don't know this, but I . . . a guy broke in through the window. . . ."

"Oh my God!" he said. "Are you okay? Is there anything we can do to help?"

"Would you mind standing there while I open the door to my apartment?" I asked. He unbolted his chain lock as I put the key into the door and then gingerly kicked it open. I let it swing wide so I could see inside without having to actually enter. The first thing I noticed was that my power tools were still lying on my worktable.

"Oh, shit," I said, seeing something else. "I think he got my purse."

"Probably had a belt and shoes to match," said the blond guy. Yes, it was a predictable dumb joke. Inappropriate and not even all that funny. But at that moment it seemed like the most hilarious joke in the world. I laughed and laughed, thrilled to have had two occasions to laugh on a night like this, wanting to stay inside that laughter as long as I could.

"Honey, why don't you come in and have a drink with us," said the blond guy, stepping out from behind his door and into the foyer. "I have to apologize. Kevin and I just split the last Quaalude. But we still have Valium and Tuinal. . . ." He held out a faux-antique tin full of pills of all different colors and shapes.

"No thanks," I said, refusing the pharmaceuticals but relieved by the invitation to escape into someone's apartment besides my own. The last thing I wanted was to sit in my apartment by myself. So I followed them back into their art deco– and rococo-laden lair, which looked like it had been decorated by someone's middle-aged aunt who owned a thrift store. Kevin led me over to their Victorian floral print sofa, and his blond partner poured me a glass of white wine.

After my story had worn all three of us out, my new blond friend handed me a big envelope full of photographs he wanted me to see.

"This is me as Judy. And here I am as Barbra," he said, as I shuffled through a massive pile of photos of my two hosts dressed as female celebrities, stripping onstage. "That's Kevin as Carol Channing and Lady Bird Johnson!" I oohed and aahed, dwelling on each photo with great enthusiasm, happy to go slowly so I wouldn't have to leave.

How odd that the weekend had begun and ended with female impersonators. Now Charles Pierce and his impression of Bette Davis became a detail over which the three of us could bond.

"I have a favor to ask you," Kevin confessed, once he

heard I was an art student. "I've been doing some drawing. Would you mind having a look at some of my recent work? I'd love an honest critique."

"I wouldn't mind at all!" I said with a forced enthusiasm that really meant *Just don't make me go back to my apartment alone.*

He brought out a giant pad full of charcoal sketches, set it on a chair, and began turning the pages. I focused intently on examining each of his incredibly detailed studies of male nudes. In almost every case the proportions of their bodies were off: the arms too long, the legs too short, the feet too blocky, the penises much too long or too wide. (Or were they? They were, weren't they? They had to be, didn't they?)

Then I threw myself into an earnest and scholarly critique of the drawings that offered all of the formulas for drawing anatomy I had learned in class thus far. At no point during our discussion did either one of us ever mention, even in passing, that all the drawings were of men having anal sex.

Finally it was daybreak. I was relieved to see my old friend the sun on this bright new day. My plan was to start out fresh and put the past behind me. I would resume my student routine as though nothing had ever happened.

Except now every aspect of the world appeared somehow different. Overnight I seemed to have gotten the lead in a Fellini film.

I was floating above myself as I walked to class, scrutinizing my every move with suspicion. Now I was aware, for the first time, of how my clothing hung on my body.

I also seemed to have sprouted some kind of radar or antenna whose job it was to scan the 360 degrees around me for signs of danger. Everywhere I looked, I was picking up worrisome details, subtle vibrations about some stranger's bad intentions. None of the assumptions I'd had yesterday seemed to apply anymore. As I walked to the university down Telegraph Avenue, all the people I passed appeared to be looking at me through a fish-eye lens. If I caught their gaze, an alarm went off in my nervous system. My heart began to race and my breathing quickened. The hair on my arms stood up. I felt light-headed. What was wrong with these people? Why were they staring at me?

All that independence, swagger, and newly developing sense of power I had begun to try on over the past few weeks of summer quarter went right into the Salvation Army receptacle, along with my miniskirts, my knee-high boots, and my T-shirt dresses. The clothes I was used to wearing suddenly seemed like a dangerous wardrobe for a war zone: a magnet for the wrong kind of attention. Looking attractive now struck me as a very stupid idea.

Too afraid to return to my apartment, I spent the next few weeks on the couches of friends. And along with my increasing paranoia came Rime of the Ancient Mariner's disease. I felt compelled to tell the story of what had happened to me, over and over and over to anyone who dared to say, "What you been up to?" or "How was your summer?" I told it in cafés and classrooms, packaged and burnished like it was just another amusing anecdote full of self-deprecation, well-timed pauses, carefully constructed one-liners, and inappropriate laughter.

My favorite part of the grisly tale, in addition to meeting my neighbors, was the little boy in the waiting room. "If you ain't Medusa, you is Medusa's sister," I would repeat to everyone, laughing, never fully appreciating how stunned the people on whom I sprung this story were to hear me tell it.

Oddly enough, in addition to the flabbergasted expressions that greeted every telling, an alarmingly high percentage of the girls who heard my story responded with "Something like that happened to me, too." Then they'd fish out their stories as a way to make me feel better about mine. On the bright side, I stopped feeling so alone.

It was early August and summer quarter was creeping to a close. I still hadn't told my parents what had happened because I didn't want to suffer the predictable consequences of having my newfound independence shut down: Goodbye, apartment living; hello, Mrs. Bissonette!

Despite my display of bravado, I was on shaky emotional ground. Tired of growing weepy at unpredictable times but unable to will normalcy back into my routine, I started cutting classes and stopped turning in assignments.

So I made an appointment to talk to a university-affiliated therapist, knowing in advance what I wanted her to say. I wanted her to tell me that I was acting like a baby. "Get over it," I thought she'd tell me. "It's been two weeks already. Move on."

"I just keep walking around feeling sorry for myself," I said to her, trying to bait her into delivering the message I thought I needed. "Boo-hoo. Poor me. I start to cry for no reason."

"Of course you do," she said. "But it's not for no reason. You have every right to feel sorry for yourself."

I never went back.

When school ended a couple of weeks later, I had no choice but to go home for the rest of the month. The lease on my new apartment didn't start until September. A guy from my life drawing class came with me and stood guard outside the door of the crime scene while I packed everything I owned into the trunk of my car.

I arrived in the driveway of my parents' house near Palo Alto the day after my nineteenth birthday.

At a belated birthday dinner that night, my parents wanted to hear all about school. They had a million questions about how it had gone with Mr. IFAP. They were proud I had studied with such a world-famous man.

"What did he think of your work?" my mother asked.

"Um... I think he liked it," I said.

"What sort of things did he have to say?" my father asked.

"Well, you know... this and that. I don't really remember," I mumbled.

"Do you think he might put you on a list for a scholarship or something?" my father asked.

"Or maybe invite you to exhibit at the gallery where he shows?" said my mother.

"I don't know," I said, rushing past the uncomfortable. "Maybe. Who knows."

Then, after dinner, of course they both wanted to see what I'd been working on.

I had no explanation for why I had so few pieces of work. So I kind of hemmed and hawed and then showed them the only painting I'd finished: a watercolor self-portrait with snakes coming out of my hair. Beneath it I had written the words "Medusa's Sister."

My mother looked at me and shook her head.

"That's *it*?" she said. "This is why you had to go to school all summer? Anything else?"

"Well," I said, "wait till you see my new power tools."

Roiling on a River

S<small>OME PEOPLE ARE SURPRISED TO LEARN THAT</small> I <small>WENT CAMPING A</small>
lot when I was in my twenties. I'm not sure why this sur-
prises them. Maybe the endless excuses I have used over the
years to avoid attending parties have added up to the impression that I have had the flu for two decades, thus creating a
portrait of someone who is fragile and consumptive. Of
course, it could also be the detail that I haven't done any additional camping in the last twenty years.

I'm ashamed to admit that, back when I camped a lot,
part of my motivation was provided by boyfriends who were
gung ho about it. As soon as I shifted into a pattern of dating
men who laughed derisively at the idea of spending the night
in the great outdoors, it all came to a halt. I was too chicken
to go by myself and too depressed by the thought of the forced
gaiety and intimacy I might encounter in a group excursion
with people I had never met.

That's why when a magazine asked me to write about an

all-women's white-water rafting trip in Utah, I had conflicting emotions. The part that proved thorniest was overcoming a fear I had been unable to shake since getting trapped for several hours in a stalled elevator during a lightning storm a month before. I realize that an elevator and a raft usually are listed in different categories under "modes of transportation," but I was haunted by the memory of how I had heard the lightning and thunder *before* I got into the elevator that day. I kept revisiting the image of me perfectly safe moments before, but too distracted or stupid to say to myself, "Electrical storm. Electrical elevator. Burn some calories and take the stairs." Even later, as I was being pulled from between elevator doors, which had been pried open with crowbars by uniformed firemen, I had already begun berating myself with "For Christ's sake, woman—learn to *think* before you act."

This voice was haunting me now. If ever an event seemed to have the potential for unforeseen consequences requiring critical calorie-burning thought before action, it was an all-women's white-water rafting trip.

Yet somewhere else, deep inside of me, the idea of waking up in the morning, hearing a river, and looking up at pine trees rang an ancient but really clear bell. The photos posted online of the last version of this trip were calling to me like the Sirens (or their hetero-female equivalent, which in my case would be three long-haired indie rockers with sad, knowing eyes, stranded on a raft with their acoustic guitars singing carefully phrased, psychologically astute, semi-autobiographical songs).

"Where red rock canyon meets alpine forest," said the text, describing the adventure that would unfold. It went on to describe "waterfalls...prehistoric Indian pictographs...

slick rock grottos." "Yes! All the things I love and miss," my soul cried out, followed seconds later by the voice of Ashley, the horror-movie star with whom I was now sharing a head. Ashley was a likable, somewhat sensible girl who became increasingly hysterical as signs of danger started to add up. She was carefully scrutinizing the rest of the promotional copy and finding red flags everywhere: " 'It's an *investment* in yourself. A chance to *renew* both body and soul,' " she read aloud. "You want to be trapped on a raft with people who talk like a commercial for feminine hygiene products? 'Spectacular river canyons offer secluded beaches where your *facilitators* will share the ancient art of hatha yoga and the *healing* techniques of massage therapy. You'll experience excitement and *female bonding* as you run the rapids with women *guides* who understand *the nature of the journey*,' " she continued.

By now, Ashley was obsessed with the list of pretentious buzzwords she thought meant trouble: "investment," "renew," "healing," "guides," and "journey" as pretentious buzzwords that meant trouble. She was also bothered by the presence of "facilitators" and by "massage therapy" as a mandatory activity.

"And then there's the part where it says 'female bonding,' " she said, clearing her throat and looking out of the corners of her eyes. "As though entire genders are destined to get along."

"Well . . . come on! I love yoga!" I shot back. "And I have tons of female friends."

"Merrill, I'm not talking about yoga. I'm not talking about friends. I'm talking about female bonding." Ashley was well acquainted with my previous unhappy experience with this very thing since she and I had met for the first time on an all-girl trip to Italy right after high school, where we both watched in horror as my rebellious arty teen self experienced bonding difficulties with Catholic school cheerleaders from the South. The whole episode turned so unpleasant that the group chaperone wrote a letter of complaint about my bonding deficiencies to my parents.

"The old female bonding didn't work out too well that time, did it?" said Ashley.

"No, but I was a bigger pain in the ass when I was seventeen," I argued. "These days I'm much better adjusted." I paused to see if either of us was buying this.

That was when she reminded me that the trip to Italy ended when the propeller plane on which our group was flying home had two engines catch fire and another one explode. We had been in the air for less than an hour when the pilot came on the intercom and announced, "I don't know what to say. I'm at a loss for words." Shortly thereafter we crash-landed in Shannon, Ireland, where we all spent the night on the airport floor.

Only then did I learn that someone in our group had gone to a psychic before we'd left and had been warned not to get on the plane. Was this another one of those unrecognized moments when consequences should have been more carefully calculated? When forethought could have prevented disaster-filled action?

"For a girl like you to agree to sign 'an acknowledgment of risk' document that mentions the phrase 'inherent risks' eleven times and 'death' an additional seven is like one of those movies where a bunch of sorority girls agree to spend the night in an abandoned cabin even though they have heard that a serial killer has just escaped from a nearby mental institution and has been seen in the area," Ashley scolded me.

"I know," I told her. "But even in the event of an escaped serial killer, these days we all have cellphones."

And with that I began to study the list of things we were told to bring along on the trip: a water bottle, a flashlight, sunblock, biodegradable soap, mosquito repellent. I was beginning to feel an odd yearning to walk around in the dark, in the woods, with a flashlight, listening to frogs and crickets and the sounds of a fast-moving river. It reminded me of summer camp. *Maybe,* I thought, *I will buy name tags and sew them into my clothes.*

"You seem to have forgotten that you hated summer camp," Ashley whispered.

"If you need to be freaked out all the time, go become pen pals with a prisoner on parole," I told her as I picked up the phone and called the editor at the magazine. "I'm in," I said.

DAY ONE

I am so not worried about this, I told myself as I arrived at the airport a full two hours early, my wheelie suitcase full of waterproof clothing. For once in my Southern California life, there were no traffic slowdowns or problems with parking. Everything was running smoothly. Right up until I got to the gate and was informed that my flight to Salt Lake City would be departing three hours late.

In that single moment, all my tidy interlocking travel arrangements fell like dominoes. Now I would be arriving in

Salt Lake City at nine-thirty at night, which meant I would miss the only connecting flight to Vernal, Utah, which was going to put me near where the group would be gathering to begin the trip at sunrise.

This left me with no choice but to rent a car and head out all by myself for a four-hour drive through the Utah desert in the middle of the night.

Ashley was instantly on fire with the plot implications. To counter her histrionics, I studied maps of the area relentlessly during my flight. It looked to me like a straight shot through the desert. Nothing to worry about. "Once I find the highway, I just stay on it," I said to her.

"Yes, of course," replied Ashley. "It's simple. What could possibly go wrong? A single woman all by herself in a car she's never driven before, on a dark desert highway in the middle of the night."

Still, I was pleased by how competent I felt as I was talking over my planned route with the car rental agent. *This will be fine,* I said to myself as he reassured me by taking a yellow highlighter and drawing a line from the freeway entrance to my destination.

"See? It's easy when you just handle things logically," I said confidently as I headed onto a two-lane highway so dark that it looked more like an allegory than a road. "No reason to get emotional."

It was ten o'clock at night.

"Nope. I don't see another car anywhere," said Ashley. "We're all alone out here. If anything happens, we will be stranded and invisible."

"Come on!" I argued. "Even if we break down, we can

just lock the doors and wait until morning. Someone will be driving on this road during the day."

"I bet that's what all those girls walking home from the factories in Juárez, Mexico, thought when they left work," said Ashley. "You know, before they were never seen again."

"Oh, shut up and leave me alone," I barked as I began to realize that it had been ten minutes, then twenty minutes, then thirty minutes since the last time I passed a billboard or a gas station. Or anything. There seemed to be no call boxes, or signs indicating how near or far we were from somewhere.

"Did I tell you about the time I was driving alone on a road just like this when a criminally insane trucker started sideswiping my car?" Ashley asked me, after an hour of driving past nothing but impenetrable nightscape. She was now giving me heart palpitations. "Even though I tried to get away, I spun into a drainage ditch by the side of the road. By the way, there are no cell towers out here. Phones are totally useless."

"That never happened to you," I responded, kind of weakly. "You're making that up."

"No I'm not," she said. "Well, you're half right. It didn't happen to me. But it totally happened to someone else on *Cold Case Files*."

Fifteen minutes of darkness later a sign for GAS/FOOD appeared just ahead and on the right. Elated at the idea of even a sad, empty outpost of civilization, I pulled over and stopped at what turned out to be creepy little market with dingy lighting, unstocked shelves, and a dentally deficient, sallow-faced man at the register.

Of course, Ashley was instantly reminded of a movie she

once saw where a woman went into the restroom at a truck stop and was never heard from again. "Vanished," she said, "until weeks later, when her overwrought boyfriend, a mud-caked, bloody Kurt Russell, finds her ravaged body stuffed in a duffel bag buried underground. By the way, cellphones don't work at all when you're buried alive."

As I walked around the store, looking not for snacks but for "provisions," I realized that I was not only purchasing sugary treats to keep me awake for the drive, but amassing supplies in case Ashley's warnings were a harbinger of things to come. The pickings were slim. In the event that we were destined to be stranded in the desert in an inoperable car, we would have to survive on gummy bears, Cheez-Its, and Twizzlers until the helicopters arrived. On Ashley's advice, I also made a point of posing in front of the mirrorized security cameras before we checked out, to create a record of my activities for any detectives tracking my whereabouts, should that become necessary.

Back on the road at eleven at night, I now had no choice but to keep on driving, surrounded by thick darkness. It was almost like following a road inside a painting on black velvet. So of course I was truly delighted when at last I spotted a sign that said it was seventy-six miles to Vernal.

And then, at one A.M., thar she blows: the Dinosaur Inn. I actually heard myself yell out "Yee-haw!" as I pulled into the small, empty parking lot. In fact, so grateful was I to see that big green neon brontosaurus on the sign out front, even though it boasted no claims of amenities except "We have Beanie Babies," when the clerk asked me if I was Ferrill Markoe, I happily nodded and said yes.

"I could easily imagine this place surrounded by squad cars and police tape," said Ashley.

"Go sleep in the car by yourself," I told to her, wheeling my suitcase to my room.

DAY TWO

Turned out waking up at five A.M. was no trouble for me since I never unwound enough to fall asleep in the first place. But turning on the television to get oriented, I was stunned that the very first thing I heard was a guy on Fox News saying, "Coming up: a wet weekend. We've got a flash-flood watch. Be extra careful if you're planning on camping near a river or stream." That's correct. He actually said that.

Ashley sat bolt upright, her pupils fully dilated. "You heard that, right? That's what they call 'cryptic foreshadowing.' Get out of my way. I'm in charge now." Then she promptly wrested control of my body, forcing me to call up my editor and announce my intention to back out of the assignment. "You can no longer use your detached rational logic on me," she threatened as she dialed. "I am doing a rewrite on the plot of this movie, especially the second act where we drown."

Naturally my editor was sympathetic but felt that I should at least go down to the trip headquarters and get their take on the weather.

So...back into the rental car, and by six A.M. we were cruising through a very pretty part of rural Utah. The desert was gone, and in its place were dirt roads lined with lush foliage and split-rail fences. The homes and pastureland looked like postcards from someone else's idyllic childhood.

A half hour later, I arrived at trip headquarters: a small storefront at the end of a dirt road, where I learned that apparently I was the only person who watched sunrise television before coming over. There were no other terror-stricken people, desperate to get their money back, like I expected. No one was the least bit interested in my "Think before you act" theories.

Ashley stared slack-jawed at the happy campers as they packed and chatted among themselves. They were about twenty sporty-looking women in shorts and T-shirts, sweatshirts and sandals, raring to go. Most were in their thirties, with a few in their twenties and a few in their forties and fifties. The senior member of the group was in her seventies: an extremely fit-looking woman in shorts and a hoodie.

Ashley was duly annoyed. "Don't trust what you're seeing," she warned me. "It's the kind of false lead they always add to the front half of the movie so everyone will continue skipping merrily toward their doom."

As someone in charge handed each of us two waterproof duffel bags in which to put all of the things we were bringing, Ashley refused to buy into the prevailing mood. Especially after our group leader, Susan Ann, a woman with a touch of the sixties folksinger about her, reminded me to lock my wallet and my cellphone in the car. "There's no point in bringing them," she said calmly. "Cellphones won't work where we're headed."

"Of course not," Ashley whispered breathlessly, humming the theme from *Psycho*. "More cryptic foreshadowing. We should back out."

Feeling naked and nervous as I locked my wallet and cellphone in the trunk of my car, I comforted myself by packing extra makeup instead. In the event of a disaster, at least I could count on looking kind of cute in my autopsy photos.

Before we boarded the vans meant to transport us to the river, we were asked to form a circle, introduce ourselves, and say why we were making the trip. Ashley looked at me through half-closed eyes, well aware of how I hated stuff like this.

The other women seemed nice enough. Thirtysomething Cheryl, a married high school math teacher who wore her curly brown hair pinned up in a barrette, explained that she was here to grab one last hit of summer before school started again on Tuesday. She also bought the trip as a birthday present for her oldest friend, Tammy, who was sitting beside her.

Next to Tammy was Jody, a pretty fortyish woman who worked in advertising sales at the *Houston Chronicle*. After she'd shown some rafting brochures to her husband and he'd said he wasn't interested, she'd simply told him, "Okay, well, I'm going anyway." There was laughter and applause from the group when Jody imitated his parting words to her: "Well, now what am *I* going to do?"

Seven of us were traveling solo, though Suzie had actually been traveling alone since her divorce last spring. In preparation for this trip, she had made a special point of not watching *Deliverance* last night. Beside her sat Cindy: trim, blond, and forty, a married mother who took a vacation by herself each year. She was so excited about this trip that she had her fake nails removed. "It feels so good to be able to pick stuff up again," she sighed.

When it was my turn, I intended to be brief and unob-
trusive, since I was concerned about the reception I might
get when the other women learned I was there to write
about it all. That fear proved unfounded, but they did stare at
me quizzically when I blurted out my anxiety about drowning in a flash flood.

"Did anyone else hear the wet weather travel advisory
this morning on Fox?" I asked, trying not to sound too hys-
trical. Everyone looked at me blankly.

"Of course they're not worried," whispered Ashley, as
we lined up to board the large white van that would carry us
to our point of embarkation at the Gates of Lodore. "We've
both seen this movie a million times. No one is ever worried."

When we finally arrived at the "put-in" and each of us
received our life vest, we were all asked to make a solemn
pledge: "I, (state your name), promise that I will play an active role in my own rescue." Ashley glared at me and cleared
her throat. "I wonder in what percentage of cases that has
ever been remotely effective?" she muttered.

Before we began the trip for real, we each had to choose
from one of two rafting options: take the paddle boat, a
smaller raft where everyone wore a helmet and helped to
paddle, or be a helmetless freeloader on one of the larger orange rafts that carried the refrigeration chests and tents. The
paddle boat seemed like a lot of work. Especially since I was
already supposed to be taking the very notes that could be
critical to an understanding of what happened when they
were recovered next to my lifeless body at the scene of a rafting disaster. So I took a seat on the outside corner of one of
the four big orange rafts.

Above us all, on a makeshift throne in the middle of everything, was river guide Ellie, a woman in her twenties, stunning in her perfect brush-cut hair, *Star Trek* sunglasses, and tiny black bikini. Ellie was manning the two and only oars from an elevated platform in the center of the raft.

"Ahem. Looks like we're in good hands now that Paris Hilton is driving," Ashley grumbled. But Ellie effortlessly maneuvered the enormous raft while simultaneously laughing and talking about her sunblock preferences. If I hadn't witnessed it myself, I would have assumed that hers was a job that required a couple hundred pounds of muscle and a penis.

Our four-raft caravan glided calmly down the Green River between red-and-orange rock walls that dated back to the Precambrian period. Thousands of weather- and water-carved pastel arcs and layers of the earth's crust now became visible, some turned vertical or at a forty-five-degree angle to the horizon. Nine separate oceans once filled this canyon and drained. There were rocks that looked like stacks of pancakes, ancient temples, cars of a frozen freight train . . .

"Okay, we're coming up to Disaster Falls, a solid Class Three rapid," announced river guide Gabby, twenty-four and sporting a belly ring in her caramel-colored, completely concave abdomen.

"Perfect," said Ashley, looking ashen, "Disaster Falls. Let's hope she's being sarcastic." But Gabby looked unperturbed on her raised seat high atop the lead raft. She was clearly the unchallenged queen of this group of river guides. Rapids, she explained, are rated I through VI, with VI being truly dangerous.

Ashley inhaled sharply and dug her fingernails into the palm of my hand as we both became aware of the roar of fast-moving water ahead. But Ellie slipped our raft between two large, jagged boulders like a Volkswagen Bug zipping past tollbooths. Soon we were bouncing so gently over the churning water, feeling its icy spray, that it was kind of a letdown when we arrived safely on the other side. At which point Ashley rolled her eyes, looked around for her jacket and her purse, freshened her lipstick, and disappeared.

The rest of us spent the day drifting in a blue-green stretch of river that was surrounded by sandstone walls, towers, and rock formations that looked like the aunts, uncles, and assorted cousins of the Grand Canyon.

Then at four o'clock we beached the rafts on a sandy, pine-studded inlet and went ashore for the night. Each of us was given a bag with a tent in it and told to pick out a campsite.

Now Ashley was back, glaring at me as I realized with embarrassment that the assemble-the-tent portion of my previous camping festivities had always handled by a guy. "You're probably too big of a ninnyhammer to put a tent together," taunted Ashley from her perch atop a rock, never offering to help. But of course, when taken a step at a time, assembling a tent was simply putting the end of one thingy into the front of another thingy. Relieved as I was to learn I could do it as well as the others, I also now found myself feeling grateful to all those boyfriends over the years who volunteered to do it for me. Whoever had convinced men to incorporate tedious tasks like this into their macho display, deserved a very special citation.

Alone in my tent later, breathing in eau de musty, wet canvas raincoat, I peeked out the front flap to take in my view. Our campground was dotted with wet clothing hung out to dry on nearby trees and bushes, making it look like a tsunami recovery area. It had been a fun day, but I confessed to Ashley I would go home right then if it were an option. Tired and sunburned, I missed my dogs, and I couldn't relax because I hadn't picked a level spot for my tent's foundation. This was going to be a bit like trying to sleep on the front steps to my house.

As dinnertime approached, I became increasingly aware that there was also another reason I couldn't relax. It was time to confront the diciest portion of any camping experience: waste elimination. The camping trips of my youth had always involved simply wandering off into the woods with a flashlight, a shovel, and a roll of toilet paper. But not anymore.

From inside my tent, I could see a steady, antlike stream of ladies heading down the path to "the *baño*." For the next few days, bathroom breaks were all going to be a question of timing. There was only one baño for the entire group. At the entrance to the path, one big round rock on top of another one signaled that the baño was *ocupado*. That rock rarely moved.

The baño was the portable toilet our group carried with us wherever we went, because the state park that contains this stretch of the Green River insists that campers pack out *everything* they pack in. More toiletty in appearance than a simple hole in the ground, the baño had a seat and most of the other elements of an outhouse, sans walls. But given that the baño had been riding the rapids for years, it was to the ordinary outhouse what a Formula One race car was to the family sedan.

To make our encounter as pleasant as possible, the guides all developed a knack for placing the baño in the most scenic of locations. Tonight it was sitting on a level area a hundred yards down a little tree-lined path surrounded by pine boughs; tomorrow it would be nestled between a couple of boulders with a distant view of the moonlight on the river. After one adapted to the idea of sitting outside, alone, in the middle of the night with one's pants down, it was a little like going to the bathroom in a painting by William Turner. Of course, the scenic aspect of the baño succumbed over time to a certain sensory je ne sais quoi. "You learn not to look or think," Gabby explained about performing baño duty, which included cleaning and transport. "I still dry-heave every day."

Tonight's baño contemplation was interrupted by Susan Ann, a saltier version of the middle-aged Joan Baez, now more New Age priestess than ethereal psychedelic flower child. She was calling for the group to join her in a circle down at the beach. Since the baño was a dream that had yet to materialize for me, I headed down to Susan Ann's gathering in time to hear her open with the sentence "I really like circles."

"The power of the world works in a circle," she went on. "Everything tries to be round."

"I don't want to rain on your circular parade," I restrained myself from saying, "but what about a pine tree? What about cactus needles and pine needles? What about a snake?"

"We're going to be talking a lot about the four-fold path," she continued. "Things come in fours. For instance, we have four rafts." *Hmm, interesting,* I was thinking. *And I have four dogs. But body parts come in twos: eyes, ears, kidneys, all in pairs. And fingers and toes come in tens, unless there's a power-saw accident. Beers come in sixes. Buns come in eights. Bees and schools of fish come in hundreds or thousands. In fact, what DOES come in fours besides our rafts and my dogs?* But I kept my mouth shut. No point in getting into a discussion knowing that at just the right minute I was going to have to make a break and race for the baño. Also, the view of the river and the red rock wall behind it was spectacular at sunset. The colors were glorious, and Susan Ann seemed like a very nice person. For her sake, I hoped that things did in fact come in fours and were trying to be round.

DAY THREE

I didn't sleep too well in my mildewy, rock-bottomed, forty-five-degree-angle tent. I was up all night with a numb lower back and a leg cramp. Ashley, who spent the night with me, pleaded with me not to take a midnight hike to the baño. Starting at about two in the morning, she began babbling about how the campsite might be haunted, using the wet clothes hanging on the trees and blowing about in the moonlight as visual proof of the presence of an unseen dimension.

After a night of listening to her weird conjectures, I was a little unnerved to be officially awakened at seven A.M. by Rebecca, one of our river guides, improvising a spooky atonal melody on her recorder. For a moment I was concerned about this eerie new turn in the soundtrack, until she announced that a morning meditation session on the beach would be followed by coffee and fresh fruit. "Wow," I said to Ashley, "it's fun to have someone plan all your activities for you." Even if they did start off with Susan Ann, sitting cross-legged, eyes closed, requesting in a hushed voice that we all "be the river."

"Relax your facial muscles," Susan Ann chanted as she

led the group meditation. "Relax your neck. Relax your stomach muscles."

"Not till I get back from the baño," I wanted to tell her.

As uncomfortable as I was, I was not at all prepared for Cindy to begin sobbing. "When you told us to release our stomach muscles, it really got to me," she told the group. "The way we spend our days with our stomach muscles all tightly restricted by our pantyhose and everything." This certainly didn't describe the life I'd been living, but it gave me more empathy for Cindy. Wherever she worked, I was glad I didn't work there.

A basic yoga class followed, then another amazing meal somehow prepared on-site by the river girls. Quiche! Fresh muffins! Fresh-brewed coffee! This stuff materialized magically. And by eleven we were back on the river.

Fran, an aspiring physical therapist when she wasn't leading a raft brigade, was the chief navigator today, a task she seemed to handle effortlessly. "These all-women's trips are very different from the usual mixed-gender ones," she told me while she led four rafts down a river, "because the women act more like themselves without men and children to caretake." To be sure, I had noticed a very relaxed, uninhibited, less-vain-than-usual vibe among the ladies. Especially the heavy women in minimum-coverage bikinis letting it all hang out. I watched in awe as one unashamedly picked whole peanuts out of a bag of trail mix and pressed them into her peanut butter sandwich.

Despite Ashley's constant harangues, I, too, was feeling relaxed, though I was still secretly applying my eyeliner in the morning. Why I was doing this was unclear. If ever a circumstance didn't call for eyeliner, this would be it. Maybe it was because of pressure from Ashley, whose makeup was always perfect even though she was so genetically perfect that she never needed to wear it. Until now I wasn't aware that makeup was such an ingrained habit for me. Hundreds of miles from civilization, out in the middle of a river on a raft with the extra-peanuts lady, it certainly didn't feel necessary.

After a few hours of floating downstream and staring up at the muted pastel colors of the eroded rock walls looming above the river, we pulled our rafts ashore for another four-star lunch. This time it included a homemade Japanese-style red cabbage coleslaw with sesame seeds that was so delicate I made the guides give me the recipe.

Later, we took a hike through a cactus-and-scrub-brush-studded desertscape to look at some pictographs carved into the exterior of a cave by Indians, followed by a slippery, steep climb up a rocky slope to a freezing-cold waterfall. Elaine, a seventy-two-year-old woman, was hiking ahead of me, right at the front of the line. Amazing how any inclination to complain was diminished by trying to keep pace with a fast-moving septuagenarian.

As much as I was skeptical of the whole idea of "female bonding," something about this experience did seem conducive to openness. Maybe it evolved out of the sharing of experiences far from the usual distractions of the Internet and real life. It may also have had something to do with the kind of person who chose to sign up for a trip like this one. As a group they were a little heartier and a good deal less vain than those you might meet standing in line for TV show tickets or a Club Med mixer.

And yes, the openness also seemed gender-related. Something did seem to happen in a group of women (the estrogen? the oxytocin?) that encouraged the kind of personal confessions that were hard to imagine taking place on the side of a mountain with a group of men who just met yesterday. While we were climbing down from the waterfall, Susan Ann started to tell me, almost out of nowhere, that the way she learned she was adopted was when her mother called her home in the middle of a school day. "You're adopted," her mother told her when she was eight years old. "Now, never mention this again." Then she sent her back to school and never said another word about it.

Now that Susan Ann felt she had successfully reinvented herself, I was glad that she seemed happy. I hoped she would eventually get four of everything she wanted.

After the hike, we all got back on the rafts and headed to a spot in the river where we encountered our first Class V rapid. This one required a negotiation between inflatable vessel and river rock topography that was so complicated that a girl guide conference convened to plan our logistics from a spot high on the riverbank.

I couldn't hear what was being said, but I imagined that the calculations needed to slide a big floating vessel through an obstacle course full of craggy, irregular boulders and fast-moving water had to be somewhere between the ones required to sink an eight ball and to parallel park a tanker truck on a steep hill. The tanned, bikini-wearing, gum-snapping girls who were doing the piloting seemed as unfazed as ever.

As each raft maneuvered successfully through the white-water spouts and falls, its pilot got a big round of applause from the others. Then I gave myself one a little later, after I did a better job of setting up my tent the second night by taking the extra time to remove the rocks and the branches from the foundation. Tasks involving the need for physical action seemed to shut Ashley up. I forgot to be upset about my dogs or my weight or my career or serial killers for most of the day, even if for some reason I was still wearing eyeliner.

After dinner, it was announced that our activity for the night would be a massage therapy class. And just like that, Ashley appeared again, bug-eyed with one raised eyebrow.

Shrugging off her warnings, I joined the group gathering around a campfire. Everyone was dressed in the usual evening wardrobe of sweaters and sweatpants. Only in this case, we were all told that we had to take off our shoes and pick a partner for a foot massage. This is precisely the kind of thing, Ashley reminded me, I *really* hate.

"You cringe when someone comes up behind you and starts to rub your shoulders," Ashley needled. Of course, she was right. Even in a luxurious spa setting where I am over-paying for the service, I become ill at ease and bored lying on a table while someone kneads my muscles. I also get uncomfortable when a hug lasts too long.

Still, the fact that this particular massage therapy class was being taught by Arlene, a big woman who ran a steakhouse in Utah for thirteen years, went a long way toward making it all seem more interesting, though not as interesting as it would have been if she were teaching a class in how to manage a steakhouse.

Luckily for me, my massage partner, Janine, a woman who owned her own pretzel-cart business in Chicago, seemed equally uncomfortable. This made me more relaxed.

Ultimately, I was forced to conclude that running a steakhouse may not be the best training ground for a wannabe massage instructor, surprised as I was by her recommendation that after we finished giving a massage, we should fling the person's energy away from us with a violent wrist flick, like we would a fistful of cooties. This seemed like a very insulting and hostile thing to do to someone you'd been oiling and rubbing. Kind of like running to the bathroom to brush your teeth right after performing oral sex.

But perhaps I was being too sensitive.

DAY FOUR

Here's a sentence I never expected to hear spoken, not even in a dream: "Last night the ringtail cats ate the Chips Ahoy." Jody was bitter. "I wouldn't have a problem with it if they'd gotten the Pecan Sandies," she said.

Today's stretch of river would slowly through some spectacular sections of Dinosaur National Monument, full of different pastel-colored rock striations that represented every twisting, once molten layer of the earth's surface since crust number one. In some places all the layers seemed to melt together, converging into the sandstone equivalent of wood grain.

It was an easy day, travel-wise, with only gentle rapids, so we relaxed and occasionally swam alongside the rafts. Everyone seemed peaceful and happy, especially Cindy, the woman who was used to wearing restrictive pantyhose.

Finally we stopped for the night at a little beach that had a riverbed with a spongy bottom full of gooey silken silt. Something about its easy spreadability inspired a large contingent of the women to want to mud-bathe. A number of them seemed to feel that the velvety mud had to be imbued with some kind of healing mineral content or rejuvenation properties. Thus they began to slather their skin with it from their faces on down. I was more skeptical, immediately thinking of plenty of spreadable things that offer no real net gain, beauty-wise: chocolate pudding, mashed potatoes, small containers of enigmatically named creams that sell for ninety-five dollars an ounce. But the ladies of the river all felt very good about the properties of this mud. Within minutes we were all covered with a coating of the ocher-colored goo. Yes, I mudded up, too. Had there been a photographer from a men's magazine nearby, we would no doubt have turned up as a featured spread on a mud-fetish site. (Well, maybe not the extra-peanuts lady.) But because there was no such photographer here, we all just stood around in the shallow part of the river, talking and laughing: a lek of mud-caked slime creatures with tits.

Around the campfire that night, there was no avoiding one last Susan Ann circle event. This time she explained that when she handed you "the talking stick" she wanted you to tell her what surprised you, what challenged you, and what inspired you. In one simple sentence, Susan Ann had zeroed in on three questions I had no desire to answer. To say nothing of how little I liked the phrase "the talking stick."

"Let's get out of here," Ashley said. She was so over this.

"It's our last night," I reprimanded her, happy when she agreed to go back to the tent so I could play along without further ironic interference.

This led me to another gender-related moment: leave it to a group of women to all be able to have a meaningful personal revelation in the space of just seventy-two hours when called upon to do so.

Quite a few women had been inspired by the daughter, mother, grandmother triad traveling together who seemed to be genuinely enjoying each other's company. For my part, I had been watching this reunion as though I was Margaret Mead, observing the customs of a miraculous and magical family unit utterly unlike my own. Mainly I was astonished by Michelle, the granddaughter, who answers the question "What inspires you?" with "I know people who hate their parents. And hate their birthdays. And hate getting old. But I look at my mother and my grandmother and I think, 'How can I *not* look forward to that next stage?'" *Amazing,* I thought, unable to remember having had a single moment like the one she was describing, trying not to dwell on images of my frequently unhappy mother and depressed grandmother.

Then I thought about Ashley, my horror-movie star, and her real origin became clearer as I realized her harsh message of terror and doom should have been buried with the rest of my unhappy female relatives. At the very least, it seemed like a smart idea for me to insist that she change film genres. Time to force-feed Ashley some new movie plots or stop inviting her altogether.

Back in the circle, it was now time for Cheryl, the math teacher, to take the talking stick. "I had a really bad childhood," she said, starting to cry, "and I probably would have

242

killed myself in high school if I hadn't met Tammy." She was talking about her best friend, who was sitting next to her and for whom she had purchased this outing as a birthday present. "This trip really opened things up for me," said Cheryl. "I'm going back to school tomorrow with a whole different outlook on life."

Next the talking stick was handed off to Cindy, the woman who had wept when she was asked to relax. Not so surprisingly, she was weeping again. "I'm going to be really vulnerable, you guys," she said. "I don't handle female friendship well." This surprised me. From a distance, Cindy seemed easygoing and gregarious, the kind of woman for whom female bonding was invented. "I wanted to come on this trip and be liked and accepted and make some friends," she said. "I'm trying to learn not to be so judgmental." Now she turned to look at Susan Ann. "Like at the beginning, I saw you and I thought, 'Oh God. She's going to get out her crystals.'" Susan Ann smiled beatifically as Cindy now turned to me. "And I saw Merrill acting all nervous and concerned about flooding and storms and I thought, 'She's going to get hurt and freak everyone out.' But I ended up liking you both."

Hey, wait a minute, I thought, a little humiliated by this revelation. *YOU were judging ME? Who the hell are you to judge me? Ashley and me, we're the ones who judge YOU! And by the away, where the hell is that damn Ashley when I actually need her support?* That was when it occurred to me that, for the first time since I was fifteen, I had forgotten to wear any eyeliner.

When the dreaded talking stick got to me, I didn't want to speak. But I also didn't want to ruin an emotional evening for everyone else. So I said a few words about how courageous everyone was to leave their usual routines and try something different by taking a trip like this. Then I realized I had done that, too.

DAY FIVE

Leave it to me to not get around to the coolest, most fun thing until the last day. I'm referring to the paddle boat, the option I elected not to take from day one. It was the only raft where all the passengers rowed and wore helmets. All along people had been advising me to try it, but I was refusing to listen.

I can live without all that extra work, I thought.

But today, I finally got on board. Though I'm embarrassed to admit that the reason it happened is not because I was more filled with esprit de corps. It was because I was so busy talking to Cheryl and Tammy that I missed my chance to board the regular raft. So, reluctantly, I took a paddle and strapped on a helmet and had the best time of the whole trip. As river guide Rebecca shouted out orders ("Forward left, back right, forward all"), Cheryl, Tammy, Sabrina, Cindy, Diane the artist, and I all maneuvered through rapids as though we knew what we were doing. "Everyone lean right," Rebecca yelled, and we all tucked our feet in so we would not come out of the boat as we leaned way over. The smaller raft bounced and crashed in the white water. "And forward left," she yelled again. "And right. And lean." So we did. Sprays of water hit us, followed by big, freezing splashes. We were on high alert and in the moment as the raft became a roller coaster. Why had I forgotten how much more fun it was to lose yourself in doing a thing than to watch from a passive position?

"You've got to remember not to make decisions based on laziness in the future," I scolded myself, being careful to remind myself that I was not referring to boarding elevators during electrical storms.

"Okay, okay," I sighed.

On the very last stretch of river, joke telling started. Though during the past four days there had been little talk of boyfriends or husbands, now it was hard not to notice that there was a definite cast to the jokes a group of women elected to tell in the wilderness.

Exhibit A: "Which one is real? A smart man, a
dumb man, an honest man, or the Easter Bunny? A
dumb man. The other three are figments of your
imagination."
Exhibit B: "What are the three stages of sex in
marriage? Kitchen sex, where you have sex
everywhere. Bedroom sex, only in the bedroom.
And hall sex, where you pass each other in the hall
and go, 'Fuck you.' 'Fuck you, too.'"
Exhibit C: "What's the difference between a
prostitute, a nymphomaniac, and a wife? The
prostitute says, 'Are you done yet?' The nympho
says, 'Are you done already?' The wife says, 'I think
I'll paint the ceiling beige.'"

When I got to the airport that evening to board the small plane that would take me to Salt Lake, I was sunburned, gritty, and lithe, a heartier, more rugged version of myself.

Unfortunately, Ashley was already waiting for me in the

lounge area. Bracing herself with a gin and tonic, she was ready to remind me of the high incidence of small-plane catastrophes.

"You can't really get to me now," I told her. "I feel too tan and fit."

"Just like Ashley Judd at the beginning of *Kiss the Girls,*" Ashley came back, "right before the serial killer imprisons her in an underground grotto."

"No...more like something from *Under the Tuscan Sun* or *Eat Pray Love,*" I countered.

"We intentionally avoided seeing both of those movies," Ashley said with a smirk. "We really really *hate* movies like those."

"I know. And I still don't want to see them," I admitted. "But I think for both of our sakes, before we travel together again, you need to sit down and internalize the premises of a couple of chick flicks."

WHAT I LEARNED

1. Sunblock really does work.
2. Do the hard thing you don't want to do right away. That way, if you decide to reject it, it will be for a good reason.
3. Cryptic foreshadowing and scary plot points don't always add up to a horror movie. Not even when the cast includes girls in bikinis.
4. Things really do come in fours, after all. For instance, there are four things on this list.

Jimmy Explains His Wake-up Techniques

It was midmorning on a Tuesday, and I had been sitting behind my desk, surrounded on all sides by my dogs. Even so, I was edgy. I had been trying unsuccessfully to write since six A.M. Creatively, everything had come to a halt. When that happens I often turn to my dogs for inspiration. But what inspiring thing about them hadn't I already mined?

Well, it occurred to me, I hadn't yet written about how I came to adopt my two retrievers, Jimmy and Ginger, after their paterfamilias was arrested for Ponzi schemes three years ago. With a posse of angry, torch-bearing fraud victims hot on his trail, the man in whose house my two dogs had once lived fled our city, leaving his dogs at my vet's, along with his unpaid bill. A friend mentioned the dogs to me because the black one resembled my recently deceased, greatly beloved dog Lewis.

So I decided to pay him a visit.

I found him sharing a cage with a reddish female counter-part in the boarding area of my vet's hospital facility, where they had been sitting for five months, waiting patiently for someone who was never coming back. There they were: two seventy-five-pound dogs, a golden retriever and a flat-coated retriever, sharing a dog bed on the floor of a cell that was just slightly larger than the two of them. They seemed bored but otherwise in good health and sensibly cautious when I opened the cage. A few minutes after that, they both became very friendly. Once I agreed to "foster" them for a while, the staff at the vet's office sighed with relief. They all knew it was out of character for me not to fall in love with any dog once I took him home.

Where do they think we're going and who do they think I am? I asked myself as I led both dogs out to my car. I marveled at how they both jumped in without hesitation. After all, here I was, driving them to a place they'd never been where they might be spending the rest of their lives. *Are they worried or disoriented?* I wondered. *They don't really look stressed. Do they miss their original home?* But by the time we arrived at my house, they seemed totally comfortable. Talk about a classic tale of death and rebirth: it was like they'd lived here their whole lives.

How did they manage to readjust so quickly? I mused. When a human being leaves a traumatic situation that involves aban-donment and prison, it takes years of therapy to get past the pain, the trepidation, the hurt, the nightmares. Posttraumatic stress disorder, they call it. Yet these two went right to the communal water bowl, had a drink, then sat down in the liv-ing room next to my other two dogs and took a nap. When, a little while later, I got up to go to work in my office, all four of them followed me in like they'd done this a million times.

Thinking back on it now, I viewed the process with a certain amount of awe. In this era of economic strain, endless war, and environmental upheaval, might these two dogs have some worthwhile advice to offer about coping and readjusting? Enough time had passed, I supposed, for them to have gained some valuable insight.

I decided to ask them about it.

"Jimmy?" I said, calling to the flat-coated retriever. From my office desk chair, I could see him lying on his left side next to the closet, snoring.

He roused himself out of a deep sleep, sat up, and looked right at me. "Yes!" he said, coming over and sitting down beside me. "To all three questions. Yes, yes, and yes!"

"I didn't ask you even one question yet," I pointed out. "I just called your name. I have no idea what you think you are answering."

"Will you come here, do you want to go for a walk, and do you want a cookie?" he said. "The three questions that are always implied when you call my name. And for the record, the answer to all three is always yes."

"I'm not always offering a walk or a cookie when I say your name," I told him. "I called you over to ask you something else. I want to know what you remember about the day that I first brought you here to my home."

"When I was a puppy? I was much too young to remember."

"You were five years old," I said. "By common dog/ human calculations, that means you were in your mid-thirties. It was only three years ago. You don't recall being confined to a cage at the vet's? I opened the cage door and said, 'Hello, big boy! Who are you?'"

"I don't think that was me," he said.

"Being trapped in a cage for five months doesn't ring a bell?" I asked. "You and Ginger were sitting side by side on the same cushion? I took you out on a leash to see how you'd act around other dogs?"

"You're talking about someone else," he said.

"No, I am definitely talking about you," I said as he ran off to get a rope pull, hoping to initiate a game of tug. "Sit still and think for a minute," I continued. "You have no memory at all of spending the first few years of your life with a man who robbed people of their life savings?"

"Here," he said, pushing a filthy rope into my hands. "Take the other end of this rope and pull on it for a minute. It will help me clear my head."

"What is she *talking* about?" asked Ginger, who had wandered over and was now sitting beside him. "Does it involve cookies? I tuned out after 'you.'"

"No cookies," said Jimmy. Ginger yawned loudly, then collapsed lethargically onto her side.

"I see," I said. "I thought it would be interesting to write about your amazing resiliency. But obviously I've hit a dead end, I guess. Anything I say on this topic will have to be pure conjecture."

"I have a suggestion," Jimmy offered. "Have you ever written about the way I wake you up in the morning?"

"No," I said. "I, um . . . I must have overlooked that somehow."

"Well," he announced, "then thank me, because I just did

your work for you. As usual, you are overlooking the obvious. Wake up, woman. Most of what I do on a daily basis is so magnificent that I'm surprised you ever write about anything else. Like my motto says: 'I am a delight to all.' "

"I didn't know you had a motto," I said.

"More proof that you haven't been paying attention!" he said. "*Sulum est usquequaque laetus video vidi visum mihi*. It roughly translates to 'Everyone is always glad to see me.' " Jimmy yawned loudly, ending with that sound of a creaking door hinge that he favors. "Seriously. You need to write about the way I wake you up."

"I don't know if I have anything to say about that," I said.

"Oh, please," he said, so startled by my response that he stopped chewing his foot. "Don't you claim to be a storyteller? Aren't you supposed to be an observer of life? How can you live here right beside me and not have noticed how like a ballet it all is?"

"A *ballet?*" I snorted. "Here's a better idea: write this homage yourself."

"You know I can't write," he said. "Come! Let's relive it together!"

He sprang to his feet and surprised me by hurling his front legs and upper torso onto my lap.

"Picture this," Jimmy said. "There I am, standing on that slippery wood floor in your bedroom, when I am overcome with an urge to say hello that is so strong that I begin a glissade that ends with a grand jeté–like leap to the top of your bed. Everyone is riveted. Will he make it? Will he crash into her? Will she be pissed off or happy to see him?"

"When you say 'everyone,' you mean the three sleeping dogs?" I asked.

"Set up a camera tomorrow and see for yourself," he challenged. "That way you can also slow it down and watch my muscles ripple. Pay special attention to how my lips flap along with my ears. Call it 'Doggy Allegro.' I guarantee: instant viral hit on YouTube!"

As suddenly as he had jumped onto my lap, he now flounced back to the floor, racing unpredictably to a spot underneath my desk, where he began to energetically, even frantically, chew on the base of his tail. "Just a second. Mouth full of hair," he said before plopping his head in my lap and resuming his lecture. "Anyway, once I arrive safely at the edge of your mattress, I gaze across the peaks and valleys of your comforter and instantly know which of the unidentified lumps before me is you. How do I do it? No one can say. Yet I have a one hundred percent accuracy rating."

"It's because I am always the lump on the right," I said.

"Nice try, but I can't tell right from left and you know it," he said. "Go ahead. Test me. Ask me to give you my right paw."

I obliged: "Give me your right paw." He just sat there, panting.

"See?" he said. "Nothing. Yet because of my keen sense of smell, I find you, stand on your chest, and begin to slowly lick the entire length of your arm. One long, slow lick from your wrist to your shoulder. It's my signature move. No one else does it. Ginger licks fingers. Puppyboy just does faces. Hedda doesn't lick."

"Well, that's true. I've never had another dog lick my whole arm," I agreed. "I'm not sure why you do it, either."

"It helps to wake you," he said. "By the way, whatever that sauce is that you put on your face before you go to sleep at night is fantastic." He licked his lips. "You should cook with that stuff!"

"No," I said. "That 'stuff,' as you call it, is expensive moisturizer. And it's not supposed to be eaten. It may not be good for you."

"You say that about everything," he complained. "You even say that about horse shit. It saddens me the way you limit yourself."

"So are we done with this topic?" I said, thinking that this was going nowhere and that I'd like to turn off the computer and run some errands.

"Are you kidding?" he asked. "I was just getting started. I am practically writing this story for you. Have you ever noticed how you always have to go out to run errands whenever we start to talk about something real? I no sooner mention the way you limit yourself and . . . kaboom. Errands. Always errands. I think you're running from something."

"That's a troubling thought," I said. "I do put a lot of un-necessary limits on myself. I should probably try to be more open to other possibilities. It's so easy for me to get into a rut. Whether it's from laziness or habit or fear, I often do the same thing day after day, and the next thing I know, I—"

"Okay. Enough," said Jimmy, "No need to go on and on. I wasn't finished explaining my special wake-up sequence. Anyway, the overture has ended and now we're up to the adagio, which, as you know, is the part where I lie down next to you and squirm around on my back. My head and my body go at equal speeds in opposing directions. It's a beauti-ful thing to behold."

"And you're going to tell me that this has a function besides screwing up the blankets?" I scoffed.

"Of course it does. But like all great art, it's open to interpretation," said Jimmy. "Some might say I am expressing my vulnerability and subservience by showing my belly. Others might claim I'm figuring out how much of the space you're currently occupying I can take from you without a fight. Territorial acquisition. Similar to the rules of football or the battlefield."

"I always wondered what you were doing," I said. "But now that you explain it, I realize you're just being inconsiderate."

"Come on! You're really going to argue with Pack Rule Number One?" he said. "'Dominate or be dominated'? It comes with my species. That's just how the world works."

"Every day you try to push me out of my own bed because of Pack Rule Number One?" I gasped.

"I play along with an awful lot of your irrational bullshit," he said. "I hope you notice how I rarely overindulge. I let you lie wherever you want, I am just quietly aware that I can take it all away from you if it should become necessary."

"And is that also why, during this so-called adagio movement, you always slam your head into mine and scratch my face with your sharp nails?" I asked him.

"See the way you always dwell on the negative?" he said solemnly. "I have never hurt you, have I?"

"Actually," I said, "you hurt me almost every morning. Just last week you poked me in the eye with your paw. You knocked your head into my face and it made my nose bleed."

"No, I never did that," he argued. "You're thinking of someone else."

"I'm thinking of you," I said. "That's why as soon as I hear you make the leap to the edge of the bed in the morning, when you start to come racing toward me, I duck under the covers."

"You do that to avoid me?" he asked. Now it was his turn to be hurt. "I thought it was part of the way you sleep."

"I am trying to avoid injury," I said. "Merrill's Rule Number One. Obviously you don't give any thought to the effect you are having on others. You're heedless."

"Heedless?" he repeated. "I'm always shocked by the way you misinterpret everything I do. Apparently my magnificent wake-up techniques are totally lost on you. Sometimes I think that trying to communicate with you is futile."

"Hey, hey ... wait a second," I said. "Now who's taking things personally? I think we communicate rather well."

"No," said Jimmy, skulking off toward the door. "It's useless. We don't understand each other at all."

"Yes we do. We communicate great!" I insisted, ashamed of myself for having taken his well-meaning attempts to share and turned them into an argument against him. By questioning his good intentions, had I struck him too deeply? Had I done something to harm our relationship? I had never seen him quite like this—dejected, forlorn, gloomy—as he continued his mournful walk out of the room. Why was he suddenly reminding me of my mother?

"Jimmy!" I called out as he avoided my glance. "Don't be mad at me! Jimmy! Come on! Come back here. Please? Jimmy?"

Cautiously he turned and looked me in the eye. I extended both my arms toward him. "Jimmy!" I called to him again, and again. "Jimmy! Come on now! I'm sorry. Don't be like that. Don't be mad! Jimmy!"

Now I pulled out all the stops. I raised my voice up two

octaves and extended his two-syllable name to eight syllables. "Jimmy, come over here," I tried once more. "Can't we have a truce?"

Unable to resist a two-handed arm extension and an eight-syllable, opera-quality "Jimmy," he sneezed, then thought for a second and trotted to the side of my chair. Once again he sat bolt upright, staring at me attentively, his tongue hanging out of the side of his mouth, his tail thumping against the floor.

"So you accept my apology?" I asked. "You're not too deeply hurt by the fact that I spoke so hastily when I said that...?"

"Yes," he said as I scratched him behind the ear. "The answer is yes. Yes to all three questions."

Celebrity Criminals and Criminal Celebrities:
Celebrity 2.0

*You can predict the trends of tomorrow's middle class by looking
at what is taking place right now in bohemia and in the prisons.*
—my college criminology professor, 1970

IN 1995, DURING THE RIVETING DAILY BROADCASTS OF THE O.J.
trial, I made an appearance as a talking head on a CNN program, where I remarked that I was enjoying the televised trial
show so much that I hoped, when it was over, some other
screwed-up, narcissistic celebrity would have the decency
to step up to the plate and commit an equally amazing world-
class crime that broadcast television would feel compelled to
cover.

I was kidding.

I thought I was making a laughably absurd statement.

But the live audience on CNN didn't take it that way. Instead, they got very upset with me for encouraging celebrity
lawlessness. Later, I rolled my eyes and made fun of those
people to my friends. I never imagined that someday I would
look back and realize that those audience members were already tuned in to the trends of the future. Because as I write
this, in 2011, I realize that to understand the joke I made that

day, you had to also understand the archaic mid-twentieth-century model of celebrity and fame that was the standard when I was growing up.

The way the old model worked was that when someone rose from that petri dish of crime, poverty, and obscurity known as "the gutter" to be shellacked by the glow of the spotlight and its accompanying benefits of wealth and privilege, they did so on the wings of special abilities they had carefully cultivated. The possibility of this blessed rise was the very foundation of our superior American way of life: the dream that you could float all the way to the top on clouds of hard work and talent. Once you got there, you would have your heart's desire; you would automatically go to the head of every line, and they would name sandwiches after you!

But the bargain you made to preserve your elite new position was that you also had to do whatever was necessary to safeguard your "good reputation" because now you were a positive role model for everyone else. The American middle class was prudish and judgmental. They expected you to be above reproach. Since everyone knew this, no sane celebrity would risk losing his or her place in the sun at the altar of poor impulse control, especially once they learned that the secret reward of fame was permission to partake of a smorgasbord of sin. All you had to do was keep the sin buffet a secret.

Back in those olden days of 1995, when I was making jokes about O.J., it was difficult for me to imagine a time when every reputation would be so mutable that going to jail would actually add a layer of authenticity and charm to a law-breaking famous person. I had no way of knowing that we had said goodbye forever to the kind of public ruin that had in the 1920s capsized the career of Fatty Arbuckle, a celebrity whose cautionary tale was always cited when I was a kid. I didn't understand that we had begun an era of melding criminals and celebrities into one big celebriminal culture. Which is not a very fun word to say. (But "crimebrity" is worse.) So I'll just call them Celebrities 2.0: voracious, fame-seeking creatures ruthlessly pursuing personal ambitions who feel very strongly that "the rules don't apply to me." Both live for attention and will do whatever it takes to capitalize on it, knowing that if they do it right, fame will be the result. And now, both categories are working with the same exact media tools.

ACT 1: CELEBRITY 2.0

Celebrities have long been the embodiment of middle-class ideals, the more perfect stand-ins for the rest of us. The big difference between twentieth-century celebrities and twenty-first-century celebrities is that the old model required the celebrity to have some kind of connection, however tenuous, to specific talents or abilities to really thrive. Therefore, a celebrity was usually an artist, or a public servant, a scientist, or a religious leader. Once the rise from struggling average person to prominent luminary was accomplished, society offered these newly designated superpeople a little more latitude than they did the average Joe. Everyone knew that talented people were often kind of weird and out of control. Thomas Edison reportedly slept under his desk still wearing his shoes and socks. James Joyce and F. Scott Fitzgerald drank too much. So did Jackson Pollock, who was, after all, a bastion of sanity compared to Vincent van Gogh. Creative geniuses were allowed to bend the rules a little as long as some talent—or unusual beauty or extreme wealth or interesting vision—was also part of the package.

Not anymore. Now a morphing of crime with pop culture seems to have created a new strata of showbiz that probably isn't going to go away, ever.

Maybe it got its start back in the twentieth century with Frank Sinatra, a celebrity who wore his friendly connection to crime proudly, like a contrasting-color pocket square. Over the course of his career, everyone learned that Frank Sinatra could be kind of an asshole. He was always mouthing off and getting into fights. He had an arrest record and hung out with Sam Giancana. But since it was his fluid artistry that made him famous, the asshole/thug stuff was noted, then shrugged off. Small price to pay for all the fantastic music.

After Sinatra came the beginning of rock and roll and a whole new roster of sexy bad boys, many of whom had their own brushes with the law. But since it was the fifties, everyone still preferred to keep the worst of their behavior under wraps. Elvis and Chuck Berry and the rest were still concerned that polite society regard them as gentlemen.

It wasn't until somewhere in the late sixties that the concepts of outlaw and entertainer became laminated to each other like a big backstage all-access pass. During that period of cultural upheaval, as various Rolling Stones and Beatles were jailed for assorted excesses, at first the public reacted with shock. Careers had been ruined by less. Would this be their swan song?

As it turned out, no.

Mick and Keith were released back into the stream of pop culture, where they went from merely successful to enormously, astoundingly successful. And in the years that followed, too many other musicians to bother naming—as well as the actors, actresses, and models who admired them and wanted in on this kind of street cred—began to get into trouble with the law for various reasons: drug abuse, civil disobedience, assault. But now, instead of being excommunicated from public life and forever tainted like Fatty Arbuckle, they found their reputations *enhanced*.

By the time guys like Axl Rose and Tommy Lee upped the asshole ante in the eighties, poor impulse control and its attendant brushes with the law had become a glamorous, integral, and expected part of the rock-and-roll persona. It's kind of quaint to remember how, back in the twentieth century, we used to think you needed to do something *besides* be an asshole to grab the public eye. Maybe Axl appeared to be an unrepentant jerk, but that wasn't the only reason he sold out stadiums. Even in the case of continually lawbreaking bands like Guns N' Roses or Mötley Crüe, it was more a case of "Come for the music, stay for the cretinous behavior."

The nineties might have been the decade when the whole criminal-celebrity-asshole nexus really gelled sociologically because, at the same time that Axl Rose was hurling epithets at audience members and stalking off with their cameras, there was a big pileup of talk shows (*Donahue, Geraldo, Sally Jessy Raphael, Jerry Springer, Maury Povich,* early *Oprah*) whose main purpose was giving the spotlight to ill-mannered people who would have had no place on TV in any previous decade. Suddenly we were seeing, at center stage, a stream of regular people who did nothing else to distinguish themselves besides confess to behaving badly.

We had, in one spectacular cultural moment, celebrities coming out onstage and in public life as the real-life assholes they may have always been in private and regular hard-core board-certified real-life assholes coming into a new life as celebrities in a kind of asshole version of the Hindu Wheel of Life. By the mid-nineties, grotesque, aberrant behavior in all areas had become as important a piece of the entertainment pie as juggling, magic, and unexceptional singing. It seemed to ring just the right zeitgeisty bell in the United States.

Here, for the first time, were men and women whose sole reason for appearing on national television was to voluntarily admit to something that, in the fifties, they would have spent their life trying to hide (for example, infidelity, incest, hateful family interrelationships, shoplifting and prostitution, personality disorders). A troubled history with substance abuse or the law was now offering a clearer path to a television appearance than an acting workshop or a degree in communications.

During that time, I became interested in the motives of these people. Why, I wondered, did anyone *want* to be seen on national TV insulting their relatives and looking like an asshole? In 1996, I worked as a reporter on a television series for Michael Moore where we investigated weird pop cultural inconsistencies. I anchored a piece that would send me to Mississippi to meet some people who had done this very thing. The show's researchers connected me to five adult relatives of a family who had all been on *The Jerry Springer Show*, calling each other vile names. They lived down a country road in a mobile home that sat on a hillside behind the bait shop where some of them also worked. The heavyset sister-in-law seemed to have been the original instigator, so I turned to her for answers.

"Why did you want to be seen on television screaming at your family?" I asked.

Her first level of explanation was full of platitudes about therapy and needing the family to heal. But right underneath that layer, something else lurked: she felt she was "as funny as Roseanne" and that once she had climbed onto the platform of any sort of national television show, talent scouts and producers nationwide would spot her natural ability and give her a show of her own. That she had done nothing at all to prepare for this new career besides call the people closest to her horrible names didn't occur to her or even matter. It was a small price to pay for a chance at a bigger stage, now that fame was apparently having a one-cent sale. Although the woman I talked to hadn't done anything that could be considered criminal—besides emotionally extorting her loved ones—I believe that she and the other people from this glittering cultural moment laid much of the all-important "asshole who demands the public eye simply for being an asshole" groundwork that helped create the current semipermeable membrane we now use in crime and celebrity osmosis.

Looking back, maybe the harbinger of things to come—the comet in the night sky or the buzzard circling the dump before we made the big dive—was Joey Buttafuoco, as he milked his connection to a maiming assault on his wife by his teenage mistress all the way to multiple media appearances, his own show, additional criminal charges (insurance fraud, solicitation, and illegal possession of ammunition), and then, after all that, a radio show called *Let's Talk,* about his recovery. Maybe we can now identify him as an early adopter of the coming wave.

By the time the twenty-first century got under way, America's industrial might had begun to wane. Not only was everything being manufactured in China, but jobs we'd taken for granted were being outsourced to India. We probably didn't even need the added push from a behemoth economic crisis to prime Americans for embracing their new passion: an endless stream of celebrities they no longer had to look up to. Americans, fed up with admiring their betters, now welcomed the stars of reality shows as a form of celebrity double agent. Obviously, many of them were idiots, which meant that you could also look down on them. But they were rich and famous, so you had to kind of admire them, too, for somehow claiming a piece of the action for themselves. In one fell swoop they boosted your self-esteem and also offered you hope. Because, come on! These newcomers weren't even *spectacular* assholes. They didn't start a war or kill a bunch of people or form a cult. Rather, they represented a brand-new and different kind of asshole role model: a loving reinforcement of everyone at their worst.

Here were the men and women you would move away from on public transportation, the members of your family you hoped you *wouldn't* see over the holidays...placed on a pedestal to be stared at and admired.

So as reality TV evolved to become the show business norm, it taught us over and over again that grabbing the spotlight with a public display of aggressive ignorance and boorish or lawless behavior was, now, *a form of talent*. To admire one of the Real Housewives, or someone on *Jersey Shore* or *The Bachelor* or whatever, was to admire the kind of inconsiderate loudmouthed asshole you yourself could easily be if you let yourself go.

And facilitating this was a complete cultural rehabilitation of the idea of the tabloid. In the twentieth century, jokes that can no longer be comprehended by people under a certain age used to be made about "those newspapers no one wanted to be caught reading at the supermarket." Ha! Not anymore.

Curtain. End Act 1.

ACT 2: CRIME 2.0

Of course, the new celebrity/asshole/criminal paradigm comes with some built-in dilemmas. After having been elevated to star status, every new celebrity/asshole still has to figure out how to keep their momentum going. But how do they raise the bar, publicity-wise, when they are already famous for their obnoxious behavior? Traditional star-making fields like acting and music don't really open their arms to these people for very long. Where oh where can they go for more time at center stage once they've had their turn on *Dancing with the Stars*?

They can try to get another reality show, which works occasionally but not often. The attention span of the public has become very fickle. So they head for the same arena that even standard-model celebrities who have been knocked off the pedestal for box office failure, aging, weight gain, or substance abuse now turn to in ever greater numbers: crime.

As every actor and actress who is suddenly not able to advance their cause through a new hit has learned, the publicity from crime is now equal to the publicity of a B-movie junket. In fact, it is better because it is more exciting to the general public. And it comes with a ready-made media platform: the news! After seeing how effectively mid-level showbiz personalities have been waltzing their way into more publicity via brushes with the law, celebrities of every stripe now have no problem with allowing cameras to observe them punching people, driving under the influence, buying drugs, shooting up, falling down drunk, and slandering everyone close to them. They know, instinctively, that the more attention they garner for behaving like thugs, the closer they will be to the cash register at the busy intersection where crime, sociopathy, and show business all collide. As of this writing, there's even a Starline bus tour in Los Angeles dedicated to visiting just the sites of these kinds of disruptions.

In the past few years, we have all watched in awe as the people who were made famous via reality shows have succeeded in becoming even more famous by going on to run afoul of the law. We've seen everything from drunken disorderly behavior and/or simple assault (*Jersey Shore,* various) to homicide (Ryan Jenkins, from *Megan Wants a Millionaire,* killed his wife), from filing a false police report (Richard Heene, from *Wife Swap* and "Balloon Boy") to drug dealing (a pair of guys from season 9 of *Big Brother*). In the new crime/celebrity/fame/asshole nexus, escaping into anonymity after doing something horrible is no longer the point. (See Sheen, Charlie.) Anonymity itself is the greater offense.

And it works just as effectively when you reverse Acts 1 and 2 and start your journey toward national celebrity by using a crime itself as your Act 1 "brand." In this model, you simply move toward the boorish, rude, asshole-as-entertainment paradigm for your Act 2. The results are very much the same. (See: Buttafuoco, Joey.)

Thus, for the last decade, we have witnessed more and more examples of an increasingly savvy publicity-seeking criminal who has put as much thought and care into the planning stages of his crime as he would into an idea for a show or a film. In fact, we now expect our criminals to have done their PR homework before they burst onto the scene, since searching for a new perpetrator's Internet presence will be the first research everyone does.

These days it only makes good sense that before a new criminal actually takes the stage with his first splashy illegal act, he has set up his website, Facebook page, MySpace page, and/or Tumblr, all loaded with the necessary photos, videos, manifestos, and blogs full of ranting he will need to launch his "brand." A good example of a trendsetting twenty-first-century criminal who was ahead of the curve in terms of working with the media this way was crazy gunman Seung Hui Cho, who killed thirty-two people at Virginia Tech. The press kit he assembled and mailed out before he fired a single shot contained so many different head shots and action-adventure photos of himself in various fighting poses, along with broadcast-ready video statements and letters of disturbed criminal intention, that he practically deserved to get a producer credit on the nightly news.

It seems inevitable that criminals and celebrities will continue to borrow more and more from each other's playbooks as they all strive to make the most of their time in whatever limelight is available. At this point, our culture has raised them all to understand that the closer attention they pay to ongoing details, like wardrobe and supporting cast, the better their prospects for being memorialized in films and books. Thus it just makes good sense for each new budding criminal to ask themselves, while still in their planning stages, "What image do I want to project? Do I want to seem playful or formidable? Tough guy or wounded victim? Man of the People or a sad, contemplative Man of Mystery? Vin Diesel or Johnny Depp?"

The Columbine killers still stand out as two who played the wardrobe card very well, whereas Colton Harris-Moore (dubbed the "Barefoot Bandit") did equally well with the nickname card. So well, in fact, that he had several Facebook fan pages full of comments from well-wishers by the time he hit the headlines and was arrested for multiple incidents of grand larceny and breaking and entering.

Of course, once the crime and asshole entertainment cachet has run its course for an individual, there is only one logical place he can continue his next act.

ACT 3: REHAB

Every form of media steps up to offer support when a fallen celebrity moves into this important reinvention stage—to say nothing of the additional fame and opportunity that become available if they qualify as a series regular on a show like *Celebrity Rehab*. And the "problem" for which they "take full responsibility" is no longer limited to substance abuse per se, since "addiction to fame" opened the door to a new range of ideas for addictions. The sky is the limit now.

If Bill W. had been developing Alcoholics Anonymous in 2011, he no doubt would have called it Proud Alcoholics

United, since no intelligent addict today wants to remain anonymous if he can get a spotlight and credit for his struggle.

Having accomplished Act 3, a special few will elect to move to Act 4.

ACT 4: RUNNING FOR OFFICE

With the presence of grassroots political organizations like the Tea Party, it has become even easier to make this last-ditch leap into politics than in the past. And as time goes on, there will no doubt be as many other grassroots leaping-off spots for political fame as there are reality shows and rehabs. Since everyone in the spotlight will also have a résumé full of the pursuit of fame and crime, neither will be considered any kind of career detriment.

I guess the circle will be complete when we see the creation of the Federal Penitentiary for the Performing Arts, a combination prison and entertainment-development facility where fallen celebrities will recover and new platforms for publicity will be born. What a website it will have! What an infinite source of show premises, political candidates, and entertainers! So successful will it be that its main problem will be keeping the ever-growing population from overwhelming the population of the rest of the country, thus leading to some kind of celebrity inflation.

By the time that happens, most of us will be celebrities or former celebrities or related to celebrities or the victims of celebrities or all of the above. But probably by then, the people who have never had a show, committed a crime, or created an online profile will be the new stars: people about whom nothing is known will be the only ones who interest the rest of us.

ACKNOWLEDGMENTS

Thanks to my wonderful agent Melanie Jackson, and to the great Andy Ward, an astute, dedicated, and tireless editor. Also thanks to the meticulous and helpful Beth Pearson and Bonnie Thompson. Thanks, too, to Bill Scheft, Adrianne Tolsch, Wendy Liebman, April Winchell, Larry Amoros, Cory Kahaney, Larry David, and George Meyer for letting me borrow their jokes. And enormous amounts of gratitude to Andy Prieboy for his patience and his very smart notes, as well as to Puppyboy, Jimmy, Ginger, and Hedda for their continually inspiring behavior. Finally, thanks to my parents, who I hope have found a way to have a sense of humor about all of this wherever they may be in the great beyond.

ABOUT THE AUTHOR

Emmy Award–winning writer MERRILL MARKOE lives in Los Angeles, California, the garden spot of America, with four dogs and a man. She has authored three books of humorous essays and the novels *Nose Down, Eyes Up; Walking in Circles Before Lying Down;* and *It's My F---ing Birthday* and co-authored (with Andy Prieboy) the novel *The Psycho Ex Game.* A lot of additional information about her—including a long bio, goofy videos, etc.—can be found at merrillmarkoe.com. After great amounts of hesitation, she is also on Facebook. But since she thinks about pulling the page down on a daily basis, check fast.

ABOUT THE TYPE

This book was set in Bembo, a typeface based on an old-style Roman face that was used for Cardinal Bembo's tract *De Aetna* in 1495. Bembo was cut by Francisco Griffo in the early sixteenth century. The Lanston Monotype Company of Philadelphia brought the well-proportioned letterforms of Bembo to the United States in the 1930s.